C Wizard's Programming Reference

C Wizard's Programming Reference

W. David Schwaderer

A Wiley Press Book
John Wiley & Sons, Inc.
New York • Chichester • Brisbane • Toronto • Singapore

Publisher: Stephen Kippur
Editor: Theron Shreve
Managing Editor: Katherine Schowalter
Composition & Make-up: The Publisher's Network

Library of Congress Cataloging in Publication Data

Schwaderer, W. David, 1947-
    C wizard's programming reference.

Bibliography: p.
    Includes index.
    1. C (Computer program language) I. Title.
QA76.73.C15S39   1985   001.64'24   85-9555
ISBN 0-471-82641-3

Printed in the United States of America
85 86 10 9 8 7 6 5 4 3 2 1

Dedication

To Barbara, Greg, and Sezza.
It really was only supposed to be a reference card.

Acknowledgments

This book started out as a reference card. When the direction switched to writing a book, I only thought I knew what I was getting into. Luckily, I had a lot of help along the way and a measure of patience from the wonderful folks at Wiley Press.

I would like to thank the reviewers of this book for their efforts. They were Larry Breed, Peter Capek, Jim Gilliam, Hollins Williams, Larry Raper, Romualdas Skvarcius, Bob Stevens, and Nick Trufyn.

In addition, Tom Pennello of MetaWare Incorporated has convinced me that this book, as all others, still does not have enough precision to use as a C compiler writing guide. Since Frank DeRemer, originator of LALR parsing, also works for MetaWare Inc., I strongly suspect Tom is correct. Thus, they are writing their own book; details are in the bibliography.

Finally, special thanks go to Andrew Koenig of Bell Labs for his many and varied trips to the Murray Hill woodshed.

Though this book has been reviewed by many, I accept full responsibility for any remaining inaccuracies. Please call them to my attention; thanks in advance.

All program examples were produced by an IBM 6670 Information Distribution System using the remarkable APA6670 RPQ (8A5010) developed by the San Jose Printer Systems Group of IBM's Research Division.

Contents

Preface

C is an interesting language. At its best, it provides remarkable access, portability, and freedom to programmers. At its worst, it provides the unwary programmer memorable experiences in program and, perhaps, operating system annihilation. Successful C compilation and linking hardly implies successful program execution. Furthermore, because of C's permissiveness, apparent successful execution hardly implies program portability or even data portability. Yet, for increasing numbers of thoughtful programmers, it is the best language, period. C is emerging as the language of the 1980's.

History shows that Kernighan and Ritchie did not rigorously complete the original definition of C as presented in their seminal work *The C Programming Language*. Thus, it is not surprising that C compiler authors differ in their perception of the language with its many attendant ambiguities. Consider the statement:

```
int  a[] = { 1, 2, 3, sizeof(a) };
```

The evaluation varies depending on the compiler because the definition of the language as found in K&R is incomplete on many such questions. Thus, no definitive C reference guide now exists, despite claims to the contrary.

This ambiguity will continue until C compiler vendors adopt a standard definition of the language, the goal of the in-progress ANSI X3J11 Language Subcommittee. While the number of incompatibilities will undoubtedly decrease, few believe all incompatibilities will disappear. This book favors the current extensions that have appeared since the original definition of the language, ones that will likely be, but certainly are not guaranteed to be, approved by the ANSI committee. As of this writing, the draft C standard is a volatile moving target. In fact, the writing of this book has directly resulted in a draft standard change, requiring a subsequent change in the book. Thus, your definitive definition of the language must remain your compiler.

This book is neither a rigorous definition of the C language nor an introductory C tutorial. Respectively, these undertakings are best left to the ANSI standards group and books several times the size of this one. Such books exist and are mentioned in the bibliography. In contrast, this book is intended to be a thorough, quick-reference guide that answers typical questions new and intermediate C programmers ask on their journey to master the language. It assumes familiarity with C's basic programming concepts and presents many tips and insights gathered from a tedious but thorough review of C information sources. If you want a book that can help you write a compiler, contact the folks at MetaWare Inc. in Santa Cruz, California regarding availability of their *MetaWare C Language Reference Manual*.

I have tried to organize the book in a way that will permit quick access to information. This has forced some replication of material and an encyclopedic format that does not always develop logically from one section to the next. Pointers to information should minimize your scanning through the book for relevant information. Be sure to glance at the end of the book for a language summary. Speed of access is the theme.

I hope you find the book useful. Please contact me through the publisher with any corrections, problems or comments. And, if you are reading this in an unauthorized, pirate, Taiwan printing of this book, may the fleas of a thousand camels inhabit your bed.

W.David Schwaderer
San Jose, California

How to Use This Book

This book contains four sections and various appendixes. While each section discusses the language from a different perspective, all sections contain language tips and hazards that should be reviewed by a quick reading.

Section one, titled C Language Overview, primarily gives language insight. In some instances, the material is tutorial because the topics are not completely discussed by other references. You may find four discussions particularly helpful. They are:

- Understanding and Creating Object Declarations

- Understanding Mis-declarations Associated with Functions

- The Relationship between Arrays and Pointers

- Structure Member Selection

Section two, titled *C Operators*, discusses the several language operators. This section should primarily be used as a reference.

Section three, titled *Preprocessor and Statement Reference*, discusses the preprocessor and each C statement in detail. Like section two, this section should primarily be used as a reference.

Section four, titled *(non)Standard Library File I/O*, discusses low-Level (UNIX) file I/O and high-level I/O. Again, portions of the material are tutorial in nature because the topics are not completely discussed by other references.

Section five, the appendixes, is to be used as a quick reference guide. Appendix A contains material on a run-time library. The selected library is the Microsoft Inc. 3.0 C Compiler, which is close to the UNIX C run-time library. These pages are screened on the edge so that you can find them easily.

The tear-out reference card duplicates much of the appendixes. This guarantees that you will always have a quick reference, even if you misplace the tear-out card.

SECTION 1

C Language Overview

- **C Tokens**
- **White Space**
- **Constants**
- **Identifiers (Names)**
- **Identifier Scope**
- **C Objects**
- **Object Declarations**

A C program consists of one or more files, each consisting of C tokens and white space.

C Tokens

C compilers recognize six classes of tokens. They are listed in Figure 1.1.

Because of the preprocessor, source code tokens are not necessarily the tokens a compiler sees.

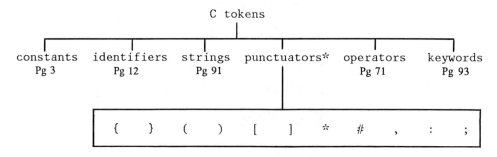

* Also referred to as separators

Figure 1.1 The six classes of C tokens

White Space

White space comes in several flavors and has no effect except to delimit tokens or when contained within string or character constants. C white space is depicted in Figure 1.2.

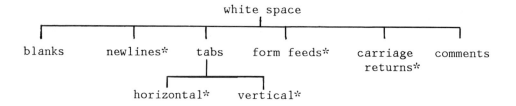

* Also referred to as formatting characters.

Figure 1.2 C White space

Use of white space is highly recommended though it is not without its hazards. As an example, use of blanks can provide visual, but potentially misleading, indications of both operator precedence in extended complex expressions and the relationship of **else** clauses in nested **if** statements.

Comments are delineated by an enclosing /**/ and may span lines. Comments are treated as white space by both the compiler and preprocessor and, strictly speaking, do not nest, though many compilers allow them to nest. Thus, sections of code cannot be logically removed from compilation by indiscriminately attempting to comment them out; they may themselves contain comments. To achieve logical removal of commented lines, use a preprocessor approach indicated in Figure 1.3 that logically removes one or more statements containing comments.

```
#if 0              /* always false */
    statement-1;   /*   comment 1  */   ┐
    statement-2;   /*   comment 2  */   ├─ logically removed
    statement-3;   /*   comment 3  */   ┘  from compilation
#endif
```

Figure 1.3 Use of the preprocessor to achieve portable comment-nesting effect

Also, see *Escape Sequences*.

Hazard:

unclosed-comments

Constants

The classes of C constants are shown in Figure 1.4.

Constants typically have the ranges indicated in Figure 1.5. Like variables, they are subject to promotion, demotion, and conversion during expression evaluation (see operand promotion.) They are subsequently subject to sign extension during promotion.

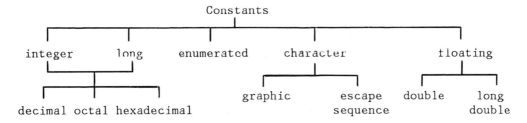

Figure 1.4 Classes of C constants

Type	Bits	Range From	To
character	8	-128	127
integer	16	-32,768	32,767
long	32	-2,147,483,648	2,147,483,647
float	32	-1E+38	1E+38
double	64	-1E308	1E308

Figure 1.5 Typical ranges for C constants

Integer Constants

An integer constant has no decimal point or exponent and obeys the rules of integer arithmetic (e.g. division truncation.) It must begin with a digit and contain no commas.

Decimal constants whose values exceed the largest (signed) **int** and octal or hexadecimal constants whose value exceed the largest **unsigned int** are implicitly **long int** types.

Any integer constant (decimal, octal, or hexadecimal) may be explicitly designated a **long int** by appending a lower or upper case **L** to its specification. In addition, decimal constants may be explicitly designated as being **unsigned** by appending lower or upper case **U** to its specification. Both types of suffixes can be used together in either order to designate **long unsigned** decimal constants.

The various formats of integer constants are illustrated in Figure 1.6.

	Valid Digits	Examples			
decimal:	0 1 2 3 4 5 6 7 8 9	1520 1520L	92020	1000 1000UL	125432 125432L
hexadecimal:	0 1 2 3 4 5 6 7 8 9 A B C D E F a b c d e f	0x3f8 0x3f8L	0X3F8	0xAB	0Xabc
octal:	0 1 2 3 4 5 6 7	0377 0377L	055	032	010

Figure 1.6 Format examples of integer constants

Hazard:

The most significant precision difference between C compilers is that some have 16 bit **int**s while others have 32 bit **int**s.

Decimal

If the leading digit of an integer constant is non-zero, then the sequence of digits is interpreted as a decimal number.

Hexadecimal

If the leading digit of an integer constant is a zero followed by a lower or upper case **X**, the subsequent sequence of characters is considered a hexadecimal value. If the hexadecimal digits have a suffix of a lower or upper case **L**, then the constant is type **long**.

Octal

If the leading digit of an integer constant is a zero which is not followed by a lower or upper case **X**, the subsequent sequence of characters is considered an octal value. If the octal digits have a suffix of a lower or upper case **L**, then the constant is type **long**.

Hazard:

C is one of the few languages in which a constant's leading zero has semantic implications.

Long

Implicit Long

The following constants are type **long int**:

decimal constants whose values exceed the size of the largest (signed) **int**.

octal or hexadecimal constants whose values exceed the value of the largest **unsigned int**.

In the case of decimal constants, a suffix of upper or lower case U specifies that the values are **unsigned**.

Explicit Long

Any integer constant (decimal, octal, or hexadecimal) may be explicitly designated a **long** constant by appending an upper or lower case **L** to its specification without an intervening space as in:

451   45L   07331   0733L   0x2C1   0x2CL

Hazard:

On some displays and printers, a lower case L is indistinguishable from the digit 1.

Character Constants and Escape Sequences

A character constant consists of either a single graphic (displayable) character enclosed in single quotes or an escape sequence enclosed in single quotes. A character constant always has type **int** and occupies the same amount of storage as an **int**. Two graphic characters cannot be enclosed in single quotes. They are the backslash (\ ) and the single quote ('). These values may be enclosed in single quotes only if they are represented by corresponding escape sequences. C character constants are shown in Figure 1.7.

Though escape sequences are written as two or more characters, they denote a single character of type **int**.

Closely related to escape sequences is the **continuation character**, which consists of a backslash character as the last character on a line. The continuation character is usually used to continue character string definitions that span more than one line. Continuation of such a string begins in column 1 of the next line.

When the compiler encounters a newline character, the two appropriate lines are spliced together and the continuation character is discarded.

```
                       typical value*
                      ────────────────
character    octal    hex    decimal           name
──────────   ─────   ──────  ───────   ──────────────────────────
   \a         007    0x07       7      sound alert
   \b         010    0x08       8      backspace (BS)
   \t         011    0x09       9      horizontal tab (HT)
   \n         012    0x0A      10      newline (NL -or- LF)
   \v         013    0x0B      11      vertical tab
   \f         014    0x0C      12      form feed (FF)
   \r         015    0x0D      13      carriage return (CR)
   \"         047    0x22      34      double quote (")
   \'         047    0x27      39      single quote (')
   \\         134    0x5C      92      backslash (\)

   \ddd       octal constant (one to three digits)
   \xddd      hexadecimal constant (one to three digits)
   \Xddd      hexadecimal constant (one to three digits)

Examples:   'a'    'A'    '0'    '\''    '\\'    '\n'    '\0'
```

* Note that the table assumes the ASCII character set. Escape sequences exist to prevent exactly that kind of assumption as a coding practice.

Figure 1.7 C character constants

Hazards:

If unintentional leading spaces exist on the line following a continued line, these spaces are incorporated as part of the combined line. Thus, a character string definition that is continued onto another line will contain inadvertent imbedded spaces unless the definition continues in column 1.

Different systems have different numeric values for character constants. Therefore, it is suggested that the escape sequence representations of the formatting characters be used to achieve intended formatting control rather than any hard-coded constant.

Character constants are used to produce a numeric value for an element in a machine's character set. However, character constants for digits are different than numeric constants ('0' in ASCII has the value 48 rather than zero). See Figure 1.8 for a summary of the differences between token interpretations.

Token	Interpretation
a	object identifier
0	decimal constant, value zero
010	octal constant, value 8
1	decimal constant, value one
'a' -or- '1'	character constant occupying integer storage sizeof(int)
'\0'	a null character constant equivalent to a zero integer
"a" -or- "1"	a pointer to a static storage string constant of length 1 , occupies two storage locations, second location contains a zero.
""	a pointer to a null string (zero byte) in static storage

Figure 1.8 Differences in C token interpretation

The escape sequences are sometimes confused with the **stdio** %formatting control characters used by **printf( )** and **scanf( )**.

The character collating sequence varies across machines. Thus, expressions such as:

$$c - 'A'$$

are guaranteed unportable because they assume a specific collating sequence. To test for upper or lower case characters, programs should respectively use the **isupper( )** and **islower( )** functions/macros, thereby avoiding expressions such as:

```
if (('A' >= c) && (c <= 'Z')) ...
```

Multi-Character Constants

Some compilers allow non-portable notation such as:

'a5'

to pack multiple characters into an **int**. You can create portable multi-character constants from single-character constants via a macro illustrated in Figure 1.9.

```
#define BITS_PER_CHAR    8
#define MULT_CHAR(c1,c2)  ( ( (c1) << BITS_PER_CHAR ) + (c2) )

char c1, c2;

    switch ( MULT_CHAR(c1,c2) ) {
      case    MULT_CHAR('a','b') : case_ab(); break;
      case    MULT_CHAR('c','d') : case_cd(); break;
      default                    : bad_case();
    }
```

Figure 1.9 Generating portable multi-character constants

String Constants (Character Strings)

String constants are designated by a sequence of zero or more characters (including escape sequences) enclosed in double quotes. Two adjacent string constant definitions separated only by white space are concatenated into one string. String constant definitions may be continued on a subsequent line by using the continuation character (a backslash as the last character on a line.) In such a continuation, the string continues with the first character of the following line. That is, the string continues in column 1 and any inadvertent white space found there becomes part of the string.

String constants are most often used to initialize character arrays. However, statements such as:

```
c = "01234567890ABCDEF"[n];
```

are entirely valid and useful. In summary, string constants can be used in any context that a named character array can be used.

The **sizeof** a string constant is one greater than the string length because of the automatically generated terminating null. All string constants reside in static storage, and any reference to a string constant produces a pointer because string constants are a special case of character arrays. The declaration:

```
char name1[] = "Barbara";
```

is equivalent to the declaration:

```
char name1[] = { 'B', 'a', 'r', 'b', 'a', 'r', 'a', '\0' };
```

Examples of how string constants are used may be found in Figure 1.10.

```
char  msg1[] = "Greg";      /* five character array, msg1 not an lvalue       */

char *msg2   = "Sezza";     /* initializes a pointer variable, msg2 an lvalue */

char *msg3   = "";          /* msg3 points to a null string, msg3 an lvalue   */

char *msgs[] = {"hello", "adios"};   /* initializes a pointer variable        */

                            /* array, msgs is NOT an lvalue       */

printf("hello");            /* printf receives a copy of the pointer to the string */
```

Figure 1.10 Example uses of string constants

Finally, note that in C there is no formal notion of a string, constant or otherwise; there are only character arrays. In C, the term **string** refers to a number of contiguous characters (hopefully) residing within the fixed bounds of a character array. The contiguous characters have a null element that is considered to terminate preceding non-null array elements. The terminating null may or may not occupy the last element position of the array, in which case the string is shorter than the array or the array has been overflowed. The presence of the terminating null is a convention that can be ignored from a language perspective, though not from a library function perspective.

The casual application of the term **string** to such arrays is the source of considerable confusion to programmers graduating from other languages, such as BASIC, in which strings are considerably more dynamic in use and size. Note that C does not preclude the creation of dynamic strings; it has been left to the user as an exercise.

Floating

Floating constants have the format illustrated in Figure 1.11 and always have type **double** unless the value is suffixed with a lower or upper case L in which case the constant is a **long double** constant.

As a defensive programming practice, it is a good idea to always include a decimal point in a constant involved in a floating point calculation. Thus, 2. is safer than 2 in C programs.

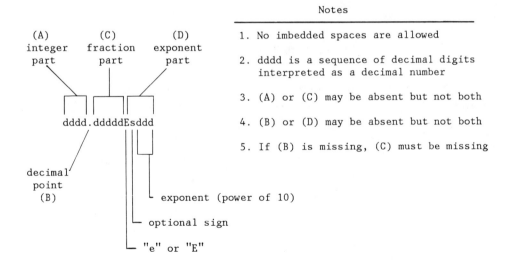

```
         (A)         (C)          (D)
       integer     fraction     exponent
        part         part         part
           \           |           /

          ┌─┐        ┌─┐         ┌┬─┐
          │ │        │ │         ││ │
       dddd.dddddEsddd
          │           ││ │
          │           ││ └─┐
  decimal │           │└─┐ │
  point   │           │  │ └─ exponent (power of 10)
   (B)                │  │
                      │  └─ optional sign
                      │
                      └─ "e" or "E"
```

Notes

1. No imbedded spaces are allowed

2. dddd is a sequence of decimal digits interpreted as a decimal number

3. (A) or (C) may be absent but not both

4. (B) or (D) may be absent but not both

5. If (B) is missing, (C) must be missing

Figure 1.11 Format of C floating constants

Enumerated

Enumerated constants are constants that are used to define an *enumerated type* variable. The constants associated with a given type collectively exhaust the values that the variable of the given type should assume. However, there is no checking to insure that a variable assumes only the enumerated values.

Associated with each constant is an identifier. Figure 1.12 indicates an example of enumerated constants. Enumerated constants are effectively integer constants and are merely convenient ways of specifying integer values.

```
enum children {Sezza=4, Greg=6, Mike=14, MaryLee, Christopher=18} Paul=22;
```

Figure 1.12 Enumerated Constants

Note that **MaryLee** has a value of 15 and that the language allows expressions such as:

```
Paul = 1000
```

without complaint.

Identifiers (Names)

Identifiers are composed of a case-sensitive (e.g., Var is different from var) contiguous sequence of upper and lower case letters, underscore characters (__), and digits. The first character must be a letter. Since the underscore character is considered to be a letter, an identifier may also start with an underscore though it is often inadvisable to do so for compiler and readability considerations. Specifically, run-time libraries often use such identifiers to hide internal subroutines from users. Therefore, it is unwise to use such identifiers. Figure 1.13 shows examples of C identifiers.

Identifiers may be of any length, though they are often length-restricted by the compiler. With one exception, X3J11 C compilers distinguish between identifiers that differ in the first 31 characters, including those that differ in case.

As an exception, the development system linker may only

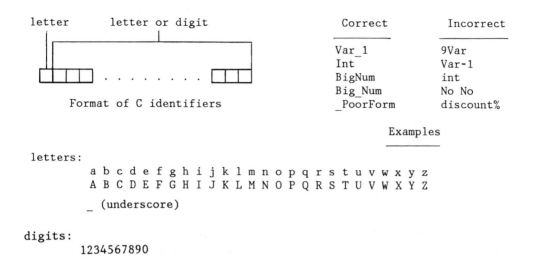

```
letter        letter or digit                    Correct          Incorrect

                                                  Var_1            9Var
                                                  Int              Var-1
                                                  BigNum           int
                                                  Big_Num          No No
               Format of C identifiers            _PoorForm        discount%
```

Examples

```
letters:
        a b c d e f g h i j k l m n o p q r s t u v w x y z
        A B C D E F G H I J K L M N O P Q R S T U V W X Y Z

        _ (underscore)

digits:
        1234567890
```

Figure 1.13 C identifiers

recognize upper case names of six characters or less for external objects. Thus, problems may develop if identifiers having program scope are not case-insensitive unique within the first six characters (i.e., var and VAR would be treated as the same objects by the linker as would tester0001 and tester0002.) In this case, the X3J11 standard leaves the case and length problem of external names as an implementation detail.

To prevent such problems, consider using long names that are compressed to unique shorter names by the preprocessor via # define statements as indicated in Figure 1.14.

An identifier cannot be a C keyword. Figure 1.15 shows what C identifiers refer to.

```
#define this_is_a_very_long_function_name fun1  /* put in an include file */

    a = this_is_a_very_long_function_name();   /* converted to a = fun1(); */
```

Figure 1.14 Compression of long names to prevent external object linkage problems

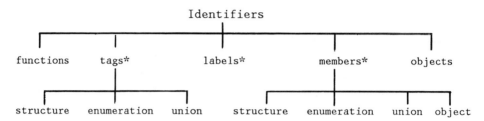

* each in independent name spaces; objects and functions share the same
name space.

Figure 1.15 What C identifiers refer to

Identifier Scope

A given instance of an identifier is associated with a unique function, tag, member, or object. It is only in effect (can be used) within certain sections of program source statements. These sections collectively comprise the **scope** of the instance of the identifier and the identifier is said to be *visible* within its scope.

There are five distinct **name spaces** for identifiers. They are illustrated in Figure 1.16.

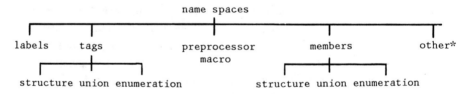

* contains functions, variables, enumeration constants, and typedef names

Figure 1.16 The five classes of name spaces

As an example,

```
struct s { int s; } s;
```

is legal.

However, the scopes of two instances of the same identifier within the same name space may not overlap.

An object has one of three classifications of scope: **local (block)**, **file**, and **program** scope.

There are a number of C notions that are related to program scope. These notions are often confused because they share a similar vocabulary that has different meanings depending on the context. These notions are summarized in Figure 1.17.

Notion	Flavors
declaration/definition location	external, internal
identifier scope	local (block), file, program
storage class	automatic, static
scope-and-storage-class specifier	auto, extern, register, static
automatic default to int	functions, variables

Figure 1.17 A summary of related C notions

Local (block) Scope

Instances of identifiers declared as function formal parameters, or within functions and block (compound) statements have local scope from the point of declaration within the function/block to the end of the function/block. Such identifiers have visibility in subsequent nested blocks but do not have visibility outside the block enclosing the declaration. Local scope supersedes all other scopes, including existing local scopes, for other instances of the same identifier from the point of declaration to the end of the block enclosing the declaration.

File Scope

Identifiers with file scope automatically have visibility (lexical scope) from the point of declaration within the file to the end of the file except where superseded by other instances of the identifier having lesser (local) scope. Declaration placement therefore affects visibility for functions preceding the declaration. The use of **extern** declarations within such preceding functions achieves visibility within declaring functions.

File scope is achieved by defining an object outside of a function. The scope of such an externally defined object is limited to file scope by using the **static** keyword. Failure to use the **static** keyword in this instance causes the object to achieve program scope by default. The **static** keyword therefore affects either the storage class or identifier scope depending on the context in which it is used.

Program (Global) Scope

An identifier with program scope has visibility from the point of declaration within a file (lexical scope) to the end of the file. It has visibility in other files when correctly declared in those files except where superseded by other instances of the identifier having file or local scope. Program scope is achieved by defining an object outside of a function without using the **static** keyword. The identifier and object location are then provided to the linker. Other files requiring access to the object declare it as an **extern** storage class object which generates a request to the linker for address resolution.

C Objects

The many types of C objects are illustrated in Figure 1.18.

All objects have storage classes and type declarations. Appropriate storage may be allocated at object *definition* time, while an object's attributes are announced at object *declaration* time. The definition of an object and associated initialization may only occur once within a program (all files), while the declaration of an object may occur more than once. All objects must be declared before use; an assumed type of **int** will be assigned in the following exception cases:

1.   undeclared called functions

2.   function definitions not indicating a data type

compilers associated with UNIX systems follow the latter convention. This is a major portability impediment.

Used within a function, this keyword indicates that there exists an external definition for the identifier with file or program scope. Used outside a function, this keyword indicates that there exists an external definition for the identifier with program scope. Because an object can only achieve program or file scope by being defined outside a function, the object will always have **static** storage class.

An external definition defines the object (allocates storage for, and provides attributes and optional initialization values). Functions that need to access the object must declare (provide attributes) the object explicitly or implicitly by using the object; in which case, it is assumed to be an **int** under certain conditions. See Figure 1.19 for an example. The output of the program in Figure 1.19 is shown in Figure 1.20.

```
#include "stdio.h"                         static fxx = -9;   /* file scope */

static int fxx=9; /* file scope */        int f21 = 21;   /* program scope */

int f11=11;      /* program scope */      file2_fun()
extern int f12; /* located below */       {
                                            extern int f11;
main()
{                                           printf("\nf11:%d, f21:%d",f11,f21);
 extern int f12;  /* located below */       printf("\nfxx:%d",fxx);
 extern int f21;  /* in file 2      */
                                          }
 printf("\nf11:%d, f12:%d",f11,f12);
 printf("\nfxx:%d",fxx);

  file2_fun();

}

int f12 = 12;       /* program scope */

       /* File 1 */                              /* File 2 */
```

Figure 1.19 Example of C identifier scopes

```
f11:11,  f12:12
fxx:9
f11:11,  f21:21
fxx:-9
```

Figure 1.20 Output for Figure 1.19 program

The use of external objects within a program should be minimized because they tend to defeat structured programming design.

Also, see *Identifier Scope* and *C Objects and Their Initialization*.

register

Variables that have **register** storage class are actually automatic variables or formal parameters that potentially reside in a machine register. They are restricted to integer, character, and pointer data types and, like all automatic variables, must be explicitly assigned a value before use or they will contain random values.

Because the variable might not occupy a main memory location, you cannot take the address (via the **&** operator) of a register variable, even if it actually resides in main memory. As an immediate consequence, you cannot directly use **scanf** to change the value of **register** variables. The benefits of **register** variables are machine-specific.

Type Declarations for Basic Data Objects

The type declaration of a fundamental data object type indicates how the bit values at the object's location should be interpreted.

Also, see *Operand Promotion*.

char (signed and unsigned)

An object of type **char** is large enough to hold a single character of the machine's character set and may be **signed** or **unsigned** at the discretion of the compiler.

Unless explicitly declared to be **unsigned**, a **char** variable is subject to possible sign extension caused by operand promotion during expression evaluation. Such sign extension can be guaranteed by using the X3J11 **signed** keyword in the character object definition. Similarly, such sign extension can be prevented by using the **unsigned** keyword in the character object definition.

If c1 and c2 are of type **char** and i1 and i2 are of type **int** then the following expression is guaranteed to be well-behaved:

```
c2 = i1 = c1    /* c2 always gets the value of c1 */
```

However, the following expression is not well-behaved:

```
i2 = c1 = i1 = 0xFF  /* i2 may get 0xFFFF, 0x00FF or something else */
```

Hazards:

Never define a variable that must contain a data file EOF as a **char** data type because the run-time environment of many compilers define EOF to be -1. You must define the variable as an **int**. Otherwise, the EOF can be indistinguishable from a character value of 0xFF because of data conversions and sign extension during expression evaluation. Also, because of portability problems, signed objects having negative values should not be right shifted (via $>>$) without first casting them to **unsigned values**.

short, int, and long (signed and unsigned)

There are three types of integer variables. Listed in potentially increasing precision, they are: **short (int)**, **int**, and **long (int)** integers. The only guaranteed relationship between the three variants is:

```
sizeof(short) <= sizeof(int) <= sizeof(long)
```

Each variant has a **signed** and **unsigned** form, the default being signed. Signed objects can be either positive or negative and are subject to possible sign extension caused by operand promotion during expression evaluation. Sign extension is prevented by an explicit **unsigned** declaration or by casting to **unsigned**.

Unsigned data types are always treated as non-negative quantities and serve to extend the precision of the corresponding data type. They are not subject to sign extension caused by operand promotion during expression evaluation.

Hazard:

Because of portability problems, signed objects having negative values should not be right shifted (via >>) without first casting them to **unsigned values**.

Also, see **C Objects** for the instances in which various objects default to type **int**.

enum

Variables of type **enum** are effectively integral type variables that are nominally constrained to take on only the values that appeared in the **enum** declaration; however, no checking is done. Note that:

```
enum x = { red, green, blue};

x = blue;
x++;
```

results in no compiler or run-time complaints.

float

Variables of type **float** can contain real numbers. These variables typically carry a level of precision of approximately 6 decimal digits.

double (long float)

Variables of type **double** contain real numbers and typically have a precision of approximately 16 decimal digits. The term **long float** is an archaic term.

long double

Variables of type long **double** can contain enormous real numbers. **long double** values are new with X3J11 and their implementation varies.

Typical Ranges for C Variables

Figure 1.21 shows the typical ranges for C variables.

Object Type	Bits	sizeof object	Range From	Range To
signed char	8	1	-128	127
unsigned char	8	1	0	255
short	16	2	-32768	32767
unsigned short	16	2	0	65535
int	16	2	-32768	32767
unsigned int	16	2	0	65535
long	32	4	-2,147,483,648	2,147,483,647
unsigned long	32	4	0	4,294,967,295
float	32	4	-1E+38	1E+38
double	64	8	-1E308	1E+308
long double	128	16	-1E9863	1E+9863

Figure 1.21 Typical ranges for C variables (compiler dependent)

Derived Data Types

Functions

Functions can only be called or can have their address taken. Also, see *Functions and Their Properties*.

Pointers

Pointers are variables whose non-zero values are the addresses of other data objects. They have a base type which is the type of object pointed to. Zero is the only integer value that can be assigned to a pointer without an explicit cast of the appropriate type. A pointer whose value is zero (NULL) is guaranteed not to point at an object.

In general, the sizes and formats of pointers may differ depending on the types of objects pointed at. It is therefore *critical* that pointers be correctly declared. A pointer of type **void *** can be assigned to any other type pointer without casting, though it cannot be used in any other type expression. Failure to declare a pointer variable **ptrx** correctly potentially compromises the integrity and portability of any or all of the following:

1. object assignment and referencing including promotion, demotion, conversion and sign extension.

2. pointer arithmetic (scaling)

3. structure/union member selection

4. evaluation of an expression such as **sizeof(ptrx)**

As an example, consider Figure 1.22.

```
int i;
long *pl;

pl = &i;        /* ERROR - points to wrong size object */

*pl++;          /* destroys memory if sizeof(int) != sizeof(long) */
                /* worse: may work but is not portable */
```

Figure 1.22 Common pointer usage error

Hazard:

Pointers with **auto** storage class must be explicitly assigned a value or they will contain random values. Indiscriminate use of such an uninitialized pointer will arbitrarily destroy the contents of memory. Figure 1.23 illustrates this problem.

lint will assist in the detection of such errors.

```
funct1()
{

 double *dbl_ptr;        /*  pointer declared but not initialized     */

 *dbl_ptr = 256.1807;    /*  ERROR - pointer use here destroys memory */

}
```

Figure 1.23 Destruction of memory via uninitialized auto storage class pointer

Finally, objects have machine memory alignment requirements that vary by object type for a given machine. A required alignment for an object on, for example, a word boundary is considered more restrictive than a required alignment on a character boundary. If the cast operator is first applied to a pointer to coerce it to point to an object that has a lesser alignment requirement than the original object, and if the cast operator is then applied in order to coerce the resulting pointer to point at an object of the original type, C guarantees there will be no change between the original pointer's value/format and the final pointer's value/format. (See Figure 1.24.)

An immediate consequence of this restriction is that all memory allocation functions must return a pointer to memory locations that are valid for the most restrictive alignment type data object.

```
char   c,
       *char_ptr = &c;

int    i,
       *int_ptr = &i;

char_ptr = (char *)( (int *)  char_ptr); /* bad:  char_ptr may change */
int_ptr  = (int  *)( (char *) int_ptr);  /* good: int_ptr does not change */
```

Figure 1.24 Alignment considerations for coercing pointers

Aggregate Data Types

Arrays   Arrays are collections of objects that are the same type and share the same name. They are distinguished from one another by appropriate indexing. In C, all arrays are one-dimensional. This observation is further explained in the section titled *The relationship between Arrays and Pointers*.

Also, see page 63.

Structures   Structures are collections of objects, possibly of different types, that are grouped together for ease of manipulation. Structures correspond to records in other languages. Individual objects are distinguished from one another by unique member names and are selected by using the **.**(dot) operator. With X3J11, member names are local to structures.

A special variant of a structure member is a *bit field* which allows the creation of objects smaller than **char** data types. With X3J11, a bit field object can be defined as either **signed** or **unsigned**.

Also, see page 57.

Unions   Unions are similar to structures. Compilers implement unions so that individual members all have zero displacement from the beginning of the structure and therefore share common memory. This is a requirement with X3J11. Beware that union members can overlap any way the compiler wishes.

Hazard:

While union members have zero displacement from the beginning of a union, make no assumption regarding the overlapping of union members.

The **sizeof** a union is the amount of memory it occupies. This can be the **sizeof** its largest member, though it need not be. Like structures, individual objects are distinguished from one another by unique member names and are selected by using the **.** (dot) operator. With X3J11, member names are local to structures.

typedef - Derived Data Typing

The **typedef** keyword allows creation of synonyms for object-attribute lists and thereby assigns a name to a derived data type. In contrast to the **#define** preprocessor directive, synonyms created via a **typedef** are:

1. processed by the compiler (vs. the preprocessor)

2. potentially more complex

3. applicable to data objects only

As indicated in Figure 1.25, **typedef** synonym declarations consist of four elements:

1. the ~~a~~ **typedef** scope-and-storage-class keyword

2. a terminal attribute (fundamental or aggregate object type keyword(s))

3. zero or more intermediate attributes (( ) [ ] *)

4. a synonym for the attribute list.

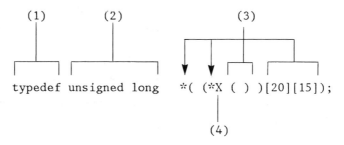

Figure 1.25 typedef elements (example)

Note that **typedef** is considered a scope-and-storage-class specifier along with **auto, extern, static,** and **register**. Thus, you cannot include **auto, extern, static,** and **register** as part of a **typedef** declaration since C allows only one scope-and-storage-class specifier per declaration.

To create an attribute list synonym, write down the synonym. Create an appropriate declaration list for the synonym as though it were an identifier. Precede the declaration with the keyword **typedef**.

Multiple **typedef** declarations having the same terminal attribute can be placed on one statement and **typedef**s can reference earlier **typedef**s as indicated in Figure 1.26.

Also, see *Understanding and Creating Object Declarations.*

```
typedef unsigned long LONG_STATIC, *LONG_STATIC_PTR1;
typedef LONG_STATIC  *LONG_STATIC_PTR2;
```

Figure 1.26 Variants of typedef declarations

Understanding and Creating Object Declarations

The process of type declaration is involved in the following situations:

object declarations

typedef declarations - pg 26.

casting of values - pg 80.

Declarations of objects are meant to appear the same as the uses, though facile unraveling of declarations can require a bit of practice before it becomes natural.

Object declarations consist of three elements:

1. a terminal attribute (fundamental or aggregate object type keyword(s))

2. zero or more intermediate attributes (( ) [ ] *)

3. an object identifier.

The unraveling of an object declarations starts with the object identifier. It is read as "**identifier** is a…". The intermediate attributes observe the standard rules of precedence. Thus, ( ) and [ ] have higher precedence than * and always follow the identifier because they associate from left to right.

Since C does not allow arrays of functions or functions that return arrays, the ( ) and [ ] attributes can never be adjacent without an intervening parentheses. The parentheses will enclose a part of the attribute list that is preceded by at least one occurrence of an indirection operator located immediately to the left of the sublist.

The intermediate attributes are read as:

( ) - function returning

[ ] - array of

* - pointer to

The deciphering stops when all intermediate attributes are exhausted and the terminal attribute is applied. Examples are as follows:

```
unsigned int UI, *UI_PTR, (*FUN_RET_PTR_2_UI_ARRAY())[20][20];
```

Here:

UI is an unsigned integer

UI__PTR is a pointer to an unsigned integer

FUN__RET__PTR__2__UI__ARRAY is a function returning a pointer to a 20 × 20 array of unsigned integers.

The above process must be reversed to create a declaration. For example:

Starting with: x is a <u>function returning</u> a <u>pointer to</u> an <u>array of 10</u> <u>pointers to</u> <u>functions returning</u> <u>pointers to</u> <u>pointers to</u> <u>structures</u> of type <u>city</u>.

1. **x** <u>function returning</u> a <u>pointer to</u> an <u>array of 10</u> <u>pointers to</u> <u>functions returning</u> <u>pointers to</u> <u>pointers to</u> <u>structures</u> of type <u>city</u>, the process is as follows:

2. **x( )** <u>pointer to</u> an <u>array of 10</u> <u>pointers to</u> <u>functions returning</u> <u>pointers to</u> <u>pointers to</u> <u>structures</u> of type <u>city</u>

3. ***x( ) an** <u>array of 10</u> <u>pointers to</u> <u>functions returning</u> <u>pointers to</u> <u>pointers to</u> <u>structures</u> of type <u>city</u>

4. **(*x( ))[10]** <u>pointers to</u> <u>functions returning</u> <u>pointers to</u> <u>pointers to</u> <u>structures</u> of type <u>city</u>.

5. ***(*x( ))[10]** <u>functions returning</u> <u>pointers to</u> <u>pointers to</u> <u>structures</u> of type <u>city</u>

6. **(*(*x( ))[10])( )** <u>pointers to</u> <u>pointers to</u> <u>structures</u> of type <u>city</u>

7. ***(*(*x( ))[10])( )** <u>pointers to</u> <u>structures</u> of type <u>city</u>

8. ****(*(*x( ))[10])( )** <u>structures</u> of type <u>city</u>

9. **struct city **(*(*x( ))[10])( )**

Note that placing the value of 10 within the array brackets is required for subsequent evaluation of:

```
sizeof(*x())
```

Operand Promotion/Conversion During Expression Evaluation

As expressions are being evaluated, the operands are subject to various conversion and promotion processes. In the case of integral operands, this is often referred to as "operand widening." The process may occur implicitly or as the result of an explicit casting operation.

1. **float** operands are optionally converted to **double**. Automatic conversion of floats implies that all real number calculations are therefore performed in double precision. This may make C unsuitable for some types of scientific applications where control over intermediate precision is required.

   short and **char** operands are converted to **int** objects with mandatory sign extension if the operands are not **unsigned**. To defeat sign extension of signed chars use the technique illustrated in Figure 1.27.

```
char  c1;    /* not declared unsigned so may be signed */
int   i1 = (unsigned char) c1;
```

Figure 1.27 Avoiding char sign extension during expression evaluation

Note that the **unsigned char** cast (not just an **unsigned** cast) is required because the character is already promoted to an **int** before the cast is applied and this conversion implies sign extension.

unsigned char and **unsigned short int** are promoted to **unsigned int**. If the expression is a unary expression, that is the type of the result.

2. If the expression is not a unary expression and if one operand is type **double**, the other operand is converted to **double**, and that is the type of the result. Otherwise, if one operand is type **long** the other operand is promoted to **long**, and that is the type of the result.

Figure 1.28 illustrates the automatic promotion process in arithmetic expressions. The automatic conversion process of arithmetic operands is shown in Figure 1.29.

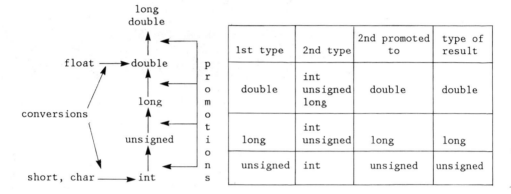

1st type	2nd type	2nd promoted to	type of result
double	int unsigned long	double	double
long	int unsigned	long	long
unsigned	int	unsigned	unsigned

Figure 1.28 Summary table of object promotion and conversion

Declarations	Evaluation Steps (order not guaranteed)

```
signed char   c = '\1';
short   s = 1;
int     i = 1;
unsigned u = 1;
long    lng = 1;
float   f = 1.0;
double  d = 1.0;
```

Expression

```
d+(f+(lng+(u+(i+(s+c)))))
```

A) s and c are promoted to int and added. The result is 2, type is int.

B) i is added to 2. The result is 3, type is int.

C) The value of 3 is converted to unsigned and added to u. The result is 4, type is unsigned.

D) The value of 4 is converted to long and added to lng. The result is 5, type is long.

E) The value of 5 is converted to double normally (otherwise float), f is converted to double and added to the converted 5.0. The result is 6.0, type is double (otherwise float).

Figure 1.29 The automatic conversion process of arithmetic operands

Beware that the following example leaves **e** with a value of zero.

```
unsigned i = 1;
int      e;

e = -1 < i;  /* e == 0 (FALSE) because of promotion of -1 to unsigned */
```

Parameter promotion and expression evaluation are special cases of promotion. (See *Functions and Their Properties*.)

Operand Demotion During Casting/Assignment

Operands may be implicitly demoted in precision during an assignment operation or explicitly during the evaluation of a casting operation. If a shorter object is promoted to a higher precision, which is then assigned back to the original shorter object, the two-step operation is termed "well-behaved" because the object's starting value is left unchanged. This is why a function that returns a **char** can be declared as returning an **int**. As an example, C guarantees that the first operation will leave the value of c1 unaltered but no guarantee is made for the value of i2 in Figure 1.30.

The second example in Figure 1.30 may fail because the first assignment may try to assign a value that will not fit within a **char**. The methods used for specific demotions are listed in Figure 1.31. Note that assigning an unsigned value to a signed object of the same type allows the compiler to move the exact bit pattern of the unsigned object to the signed object and vice versa. However, the bits are subsequently interpreted differently.

```
int i1 = 1000, i2 = 2000;
char c1 = 'A', c2 = 'Z';

                  c1 = i1 = c1;   /* leaves c1 unchanged */
                  i2 = c2 = i2;   /* may leave i2 changed */
```

Figure 1.30 Behavior of promoted and demoted values

Initial Type	Final Type	Demotion Method Used
double ⟶	float	rounding if valid float
float ⟶	int	truncation of fractional portion
long ⟶	int, short, char	truncation of high order bits
int ⟶	short, char	truncation of high order bits
short ⟶	char	truncation of high order bits

Figure 1.31 Specific demotion methods

The Compilation Process and Its Implications

A C program contains of one or more functions with attendant declarations and definitions. Every program must have a function named **main( )** which marks the initial point of code execution.

A program can span several files allowing partial compilation on a file basis. While extremely useful, the process of separate compilation introduces the opportunity for various object declaration errors. Figure 1.32 shows a conceptual model of the C compilation process.

lint

lint is a source code validation program that is useful because of the permissive nature of C compilers. It is not part of the C compiler. It checks:

The type and number of arguments passed in programs against the type and number of arguments declared in called functions (inconsistent typing).

Declaration vs. usage of objects.

Whether a function returns a value and, if so, whether or not it is able to return a value from every exit point in the function.

Whether a calling function uses a returned value of a called function.

Whether there are unused declared objects and/or code that cannot be executed.

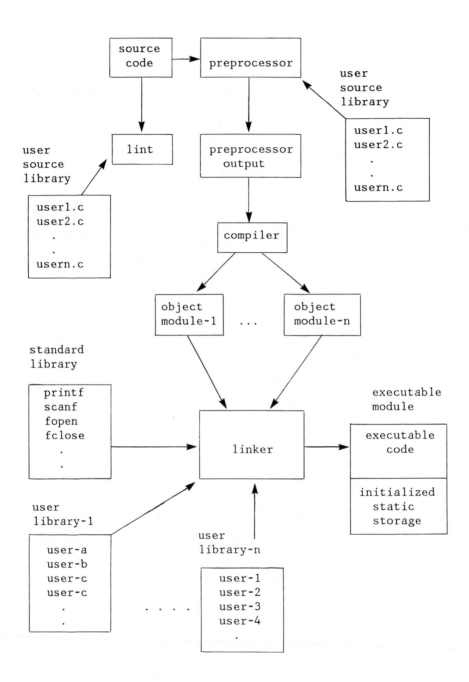

Figure 1.32 Conceptual model of the C compilation process

Whether automatic and register storage-class variables are initialized before use.

Whether a loop can ever execute or terminate.

For code portability in the use of bit fields, characters, and assignment of **long** variables to **char** variables.

For suspect constructions.

For correct use of structure pointer variables and operators.

For correct use of structure member selection operator.

For archaic syntax.

Several of the checks can be modified by the command line flags or the use of appropriate comments in the source code.

The C Preprocessor

Like **lint**, the C preprocessor is not part of the C compiler. It allows source-code file inclusion, and modest macro definitions that allow dynamic, in-line, source-code replacement or modification in preparation for the compile phase. The preprocessor can receive a variety of compiler flags on the preprocessor command line and, together with a file's preprocessor directives, produces a preprocessed source code. This achieves the effect of conditional compilation without change to original source code statements.

Compile Phase

The compile phase reads the resulting preprocessor source-code output and compiles the code, producing an object-code file. C allows a program to consist of one or more source-statement files. This introduces object resolution problems when an object in one file must be accessed or, in the case of a function, called. The compiler generates an object-code file with a map of identifiers and the location of every externally defined object with program scope. The identifiers may be altered (truncated and/or case-shifted) to conform to normal system naming conventions. The object file may optionally be placed in an object library with other object files.

Link Phase

The linker is usually a system function and not part of the C compiler. It combines all object modules to produce a single, executable run module. Various system and private libraries are searched for various object modules in the order indicated on the linker command line. The search order in which they are examined is important in that it allows a specific version of a library to be found instead of another version that is unintended.

The C (non) Standard Library   One of the current impediments for C source-code portability is the incompatibility of the so-called "standard" libraries that are not a part of, but accompany, every C compiler. These incompatible libraries have functions with the same name that behave differently, functions with different names that behave identically, functions with the same name that behave identically, as well as unique functions found in no other compiler library. One of the pressing work items of the ANSI X3J11 C Language Subcommittee is to define a C standard library.

Linkage Implication on Names   The linker is a standard system function and not part of the C compiler. It therefore requires conformance to system naming conventions to accomplish its tasks. As a result, all object file names as well as identifiers of objects having program scope must observe the system conventions as well. External compliance is achieved by the compiler by possible identifier truncation and case shifting as it produces the individual object modules.

Functions and Their Properties

Functions are the fundamental units of any C program. They can occur in any order in a file or program but cannot span files. Functions exist on a peer basis; their definitions cannot be nested (embedded). As a direct consequence, all C functions are external objects having program scope unless otherwise declared as **static**. **extern** and **static** are the only scope-and-storage-class specifiers that can be applied to a function declaration. While the called function can generate any number of side effects, it can **return** at most one value or object.

There is always one function named **main( )** which is the first function executed. Functions can call themselves (be recursive) and, provided the obvious possibility of infinite recursion is addressed, can even call **main( )** if necessary. Each time a function is called, it receives a new set of automatic objects and formal parameters.

Invoking Functions

When functions are called, they are optionally passed multiple parameters as indicated in Figure 1.33. X3J11 allows structures to be passed to and returned from functions. Arrays can never be passed unless they are structure members.

```
type fun1();   /* predeclare all functions */

    fun1(expr1, expr2, expr3,....,expr-n);
```

Figure 1.33 Anatomy of a function call

Note the following:

1.   The actual parameters are expressions and therefore subject to the standard promotion process discussed earlier. A parameter that is **char** or **short** is promoted to **int**. A float parameter is promoted to **double**.

2.   If the called function is declared externally (outside every function), then its type need not be declared and will default to **int**. If the called function is declared within a calling function, the type is necessary in the function predeclaration to distinguish it from being an executable statement, though the type is absent in the call. See Figure 1.34.

3.   The predeclaration is not necessary if the called function is in the same file and lexically (positionally) precedes the call, or if it returns an **int**.

4.   The commas in the function call are separators, not comma operators. Thus, no order of evaluation is guaranteed.

```
char fun1();  /* declared externally  */
fun2();       /* defaults to type int; fun2 not called because external */

fun3()
{
  int fun4();  /* int declaration is required to avoid fun4 being called */
  fun5();      /* no type declaration ==> fun5 is called because internal */
        . . . . . . . . . . . . . . . . . . . . . .
}
```

Figure 1.34 External and Internal declarations of functions

Since C is a "call by value" language, the values of the promoted, actual parameters are copied to an appropriate area of memory, typically a machine stack, and the invoked function is given access to the area. The images of the original values become the values of the formal parameters and the called function is free to use them as required. Any changes to the image do not affect the value of the original, actual parameters.

Anatomy of a Function Definition

In Figure 1.35, note the following:

1. The absent semicolon on the function definition line is used by the compiler to sense that a function is being defined, not executed or predeclared. Declarations of functions always require terminating semicolons.

2. The formal parameters (function arguments) can be considered to be local automatic variables that have been initialized by the function call. Thus, attempted initialization of the arguments is illegal and their identifiers may also appear in other functions without conflict.

3. The function variables (defined within the block) can be initialized by assignment expressions involving the formal parameters.

4. The left-most dimension is not required on a multi-dimensional formal parameter array declaration. The other ones are.

continued

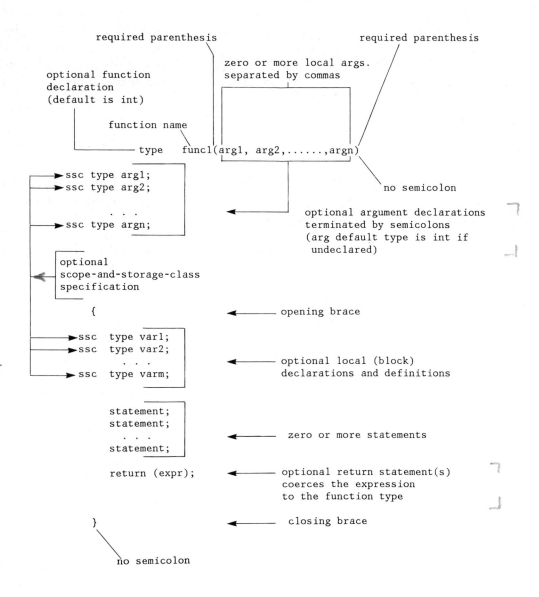

Figure 1.35 Anatomy of a function definition

5. If an actual parameter is a **char** or a **short**, it is promoted to an **int** and arrives as an **int**. You may declare the argument to be either an **int** or a **char** and the function should not be impacted. The same is true for **float**s if they are automatically promoted to **double**s. Such arguments can be declared either as **float**s or **double**s.

6. If a formal parameter is not declared, it will default to type **int**.

Hazard:

In pre-X3J11 compilers, an attempt to declare the formal parameters after the opening brace results in all formal parameters defaulting to type **int** and immediately being overridden in scope by the incorrectly defined corresponding set of local automatic variables containing random values. X3J11 compilers will report an error in this situation.

Actual and Formal Parameters

Though C is a "call by value," not a "call by reference" language, "call by reference" can be simulated by passing pointers. In this case, the original value of the passed pointer remains unchangeable, though the object it points to is changeable.

Generally, there is no run-time correlation of function argument variable counts or declarations. This is a job for **lint** or the new X3J11 optional prototype facility. The **cast** operator is an excellent vehicle to coerce an expression's value to the desired data type for parameter passing. Functions may not be passed to other functions but pointers to functions can be passed as illustrated in Figure 1.35.1.

```
int fun2();         /* not required if fun2 defined earlier   */

main ()
{ fun1(fun2); }    /* function name is a function pointer     */

fun1(fun)
int (*fun)();      /* declare pointer to function             */
{ (*fun)(3); }     /* execute the function, pass it a three   */

fun2(a)            /* dummy example function to be executed   */
   int a;
{ return (a); }
```

Figure 1.35.1 Passing a function pointer

Return Values

A function returns one result at most but can cause multiple side effects. Functions observe the normal declaration rules discussed in the section entitled *Understanding and Creating Object Declarations*. Undeclared functions automatically default to type **int**. Functions cannot return functions or arrays but can return pointers to functions and arrays. "Falling off the end of a function" results in a default **return** statement being executed. This does not guarantee program correctness.

Hazards:

1. Because:

    ```
    sizeof(int) == sizeof(any pointer)
    ```

    is true for many machines, there are many programs that return object pointers from undeclared functions that subsequently default to type **int** because they are not explicitly declared. This is not portable and K&R specifically warns against this situation. Again, make it a practice to *declare ALL functions*.

2. Never return a pointer to any automatic variable or object.

Mis-Declarations Associated with Functions

Two common mis-declarations are associated with functions. They are argument mismatches and function mis-declarations.

Argument Mismatches Argument mismatches occur as a result of a calling function passing a different type object than is expected by the called function and may occur undetected by the compiler even among functions in the same file. The object type in conflict may vary in one or more attributes (size, signed vs. unsigned, pointer type, etc.) resulting in a mis-communication between the calling and called function.

In the case of object size conflict, the shape of the passed parameter area is misinterpreted as illustrated in Figure 1.36. In the case of signed vs. unsigned conflicts, the called function interprets the received object's bit pattern differently than was intended by the calling function. In general, argument mis-declarations are as difficult to discover as they are easy to make. Use **lint** to minimize such errors.

```
CallingFun()                         CalledFun(a, b, c, d)
{                                    int a, b, c, d;      /* ERROR */
 double d1, d2;                      {
 float  f1, f2;                         return(a + b + c + d);
                                     }
 CalledFun(d1, d2, f1, f2);
}
```

			Assumed Shape of Passed
			Parameter Area Based on
Actual	Intended Shape of	Formal	Formal Parameter
Parm.	Passed Parameter Area	Parm.	Declarations

Actual Parm.	Displacement	Intended Shape of Passed Parameter Area	Formal Parm.	Displacement	Assumed Shape
d1	+0	A B C D E F G H	a	+0	A B
d2	+8	I J K L M N O P	b	+2	C D
f1	+16	Q R S T	c	+4	E F
f2	+20	U V W X	d	+6	G H

```
        ↑                                  ↑
        └─actual parameter                 └── assumed formal
          displacement                         parameter
          in passed                            displacement in
          parameter area                       passed parameter
                                               area
```

Note: The actual size of objects varies with compilers.

Figure 1.36 The conceptual effect of argument size mismatches, each letter corresponding to a byte

To address argument mismatch problems, X3J11 provides **function prototyping** as an option. In this approach, a function and the type of its arguments can be declared. As an example, a function can be declared as:

```
char *function1(* char, **int[3], int *());
```

In the event that a function call attempts to pass an actual parameter of the incorrect type, then the compiler can cast the parameter to the correct type automatically or otherwise indicate an error.

If a function has no formal parameters, this is indicated by a declaration such as:

```
char *function3(void);
```

Function Mis-Declarations Like parameter mismatches, function mis-declarations can be due to object size, sign, and other attribute mismatches. If a calling function does not predeclare the type of the function being called, and if the called function does not lexically precede the calling function in the file, the function type will default to **int**.

Called functions can return at most one value, typically via machine registers. If the calling function has explicitly or implicitly mis-typed the called function and if the called function is the same source file as the calling function, the compiler will typically detect and report the error at compile time.

Alternately, if the calling function has mis-typed the called function and if the called function is in a source file other than the calling function, the compiler will not detect the function mis-typing and will generate compiled code for the calling function that incorrectly examines the machine registers for the returned value.

Even if the returned value is immediately cast to a correct type, the damage is already complete; the registers will be incorrectly accessed to provide invalid data to the casting function. Worse, the error may only intermittently appear as indicated in Figure 1.37.

Hazard:

Declare *all* functions and use **lint** if at all possible.

Alternately, insure ALL functions return **int** values and use side effects to set other values.

Pointers and Their Maintenance

A pointer is an entity whose value is the address of an object. There are pointer variables and pointers that are automatically

File 1	File 2

```
long CalledFun(v1)              CallingFun()
{       /* v1 defaults to int */ {
  return( (long) v1 * v1 );         long n1;

}                                   /* CalledFun defaults to int below */

                                    n1 = (long) CalledFun(9224);
   >register A  AAAAAAAA          }
   >register B  BBBBBBBB

                                      register X  XXXXXXXX
```

In CalledFun(), the compiler loads two registers, A and B, with the return value because the function is declared as type long and two registers are required to hold a long on this hypothetical machine. The high order bits go into register A, and the low order bits go into register B.

In CallingFun(), CalledFun() defaults to int because CalledFun() is in another file (file1) and is not predeclared in file2 before it is called. Thus, the compiler accesses register X for a returned value. If register B and X are the same register, then the function call will coincidentally work for returned values less than the maximum int. Note that the attempted casting in CallingFun() is ineffective.

Figure 1.37 The conceptual effect of function mis-declarations

generated by the compiler to evaluate array expressions. Any pointer value (variable or expression) can be subscripted. The subscript resolution will be evaluated by pointer arithmetic that is scaled by the size of the object to which the pointer is declared to point. The process of accessing an object through a pointer is referred to as **indirection**.

Pointers may be incremented, decremented, and assigned new values; zero is the only integer that can be assigned to a pointer without an explicit cast. They may be compared to, tested for equality, and even subtracted from other pointers (both pointing to a common array). A pointer's address may be taken by the **address** operator. A pointer whose value is NULL (cast from the constant zero) is guaranteed not to point to anything.

Contrary to popular understanding, pointer sizes on some machines vary by the type of object pointed to. Moreover, even if pointer sizes are the same size for different objects, their internal structure may be different, again depending on the particular type of object pointed to. Hence, it is inadvisable to indiscriminately point pointers at varying types of objects and expect portable or even correct results. When it comes to pointers, your code must be impeccable.

As an example, you should always coerce (via the **cast** operator) returned pointer values from memory allocation functions to an appropriate type pointer *before* using the values in any expression, including immediate pointer assignment. This is because some compilers do not automatically perform the assignment and necessary pointer conversion.

Indeed, the defensive practice of implicit coercion may result in a transformation of and/or size adjustment to the returned value, necessary for correct utilization of the pointer value as well as for keeping **lint** from complaining. It is therefore *critical* that pointers be correctly declared and rigorously attended to during assignment operations.

Failure to declare a pointer variable **ptrx** correctly or to maintain the variable correctly may compromise the integrity and portability of any or all of the following operations, resulting in generally lethal errors:

1. object assignment and referencing including promotion, demotion, conversion and sign extension.

2. pointer arithmetic (scaling)

3. structure/union member selection

4. evaluation of an expression such as **sizeof(ptrx)**

Pointer Arithmetic

If **n** is an integer expression and **t__ptr** is declared to point at an object of type **t** then:

```
t_ptr + n
```

is considered to be a pointer to an object of type **t** that is located:

```
n * (sizeof(t))
```

memory locations from where **t__ptr** points. Similarly, if an integer value is added to a pointer variable, then the pointer is advanced a corresponding number of objects from its initial target location.

Moreover, if **t__ptr1** and **t__ptr2** are both declared to point at elements of an array of type **t**, then:

```
(t_ptr1 - t_ptr2) /* t_ptr1 and t_ptr2 better point to the same array */
```

is evaluated as the difference of the two pointer values divided by:

```
sizeof(t)
```

The result corresponds to the distance between the memory locations pointed to by the two pointers, expressed in terms of objects of type **t**.

There can be a difference in speed using pointer arithmetic rather than array indexing. In addition, while pointer arithmetic is closely associated with array indexing, it is possible to construct programs to do things that cannot be written as pure array expressions. The reverse is not true because indexing is defined in terms of pointer arithmetic. As an example, consider:

```
for ( i = 0; i < n; i++)
    a[i] = i;                    /* using array indexing */
```

as compared to:

```
p = a;
for ( i = 0; i < n; i++)
    *p++ = i;                    /* using pointer */
```

The first example is often faster than the second. But the second could be rewritten as:

```
for ( i = 0; i < n; i++)
    *(a+i) = i;                  /* using pointer */
```

with no speed degradation on most implementations.

Pointers to Fundamental Objects

If **t__ptr** is declared to point at an object of type **t** and points at **t1**, which is an object of type **t**, then **(*t__ptr)** may be substituted for **t1** in any expression.

Pointers to Pointers

Pointers can point to other pointers as indicated in Figure 1.38. The illustrated concepts are extendable to more levels of indirection to objects of different types such as:

$$\text{long } ***(x[10])$$

where **sizeof(x)**, **sizeof(x[1])**, **sizeof(*(x[1]))**, **sizeof(**(x[1]))**, and **sizeof(***(x[1]))** provide varying results.

```
float    f1 = 1520;
float   *f_ptr = &f1;          /*  sets f_ptr, not *f_ptr          */
    . . .
float **f_ptr_to_ptr = &f_ptr;  /*  sets f_ptr_to_ptr, not **f_ptr_to ptr  */
```

```
                                                        **f_ptr_to_ptr
                              *f_ptr_to_ptr               *f_ptr
     f_ptr_to_ptr              f_ptr                        f1
  ┌──────────────┐        ┌──────────────┐        ┌──────────────────────┐
  │    2AFA      │        │    2AF0      │        │        1520          │
  └──────────────┘        └──────────────┘        └──────────────────────┘

      3D2C                    2AFA                    2AF0        Memory Location
```

```
Note: sizeof(**f_ptr_to_ptr), sizeof(*f_ptr_to_ptr), and sizeof(f_ptr_to_ptr)
generally all yield different values that correspond to the size of the object
at the respective level of indirection.
```

Figure 1.38 Multiple levels of indirection using hypothetical addresses

For more discussion on multiple levels of indirection, see the section titled *The Relationship between Arrays and Pointers*.

Pointers to Structures

If **ptr** is declared to be a pointer to a structure of type **t** and **s** is a structure of type **t** then provided **ptr** points at **s**, whenever **s** appears in an expression (note the accompanying dot operator), it may be replaced by either **(*ptr)** or **ptr − >**. In the case of **(*ptr)**, this is just one more instance of the general behavior of pointers.

The pointer **ptr** can be set to point to **s** by the statements:

```
struct t   s, *ptr;

        ptr = &s;     /* set the pointer to point to s */
```

Pointers to Functions

If **fun__ptr1** is declared to be a pointer to a function of type **t** and **fun1( )** is a function of type **t** then provided **fun__ptr1** points at **fun1( )**, **fun1** can be called by **fun1( )** or by **(*fun1__ptr1)( )**.

The pointer **fun__ptr1** can be set to point to **fun1( )** by the statements shown in Figure 1.39.

```
example()
{
    t   fun1();               /*  declare the function (if necessary)  */
    t   (*fun_ptr1)();        /*  declare the pointer, note parentheses */

        fun_ptr1 = fun1;      /*  set fun_ptr1 to point at fun1         */
        (*fun_ptr1) (a,b,c);  /*  execute fun1 with required parameters */
}

t fun1(x, y, z)               /*  x, y, and z default to int            */
{
    return (x + y + z);
}
```

Figure 1.39 Executing a function indirectly via a pointer

Arrays

Arrays are collections of objects of the same type that share a common name. The individual array objects, called **elements**, are distinguished from one another by their unique position within the array.

An array is declared with the use of the bracket separators **[ ]**. The array base-element type is also indicated in the declaration. The array may be explicitly dimensioned by placing a constant or constant expression within the brackets; expressions involving variables or floating constants are expressly prohibited. Thus, dynamic-sized arrays cannot be declared, though they can be created and manipulated using dynamic memory calls (if necessary) and pointer techniques. Use of the brackets therefore implies a notion of non-dynamics.

When a dimension of an array is defined, the number in brackets is the number of elements in that dimension of the array, not the largest allowable subscript in that dimension.

All C arrays are single-dimensional. C emulates multi-dimensional arrays by treating them as arrays whose individual elements are or may be arrays, etc. Consider the array definition:

```
static int i[2][3][2] = { 0, 1, 2, 3, 4, 5, 6, 7, 8, 9, 10, 11 };
```

This defines an array **i** that has two elements **i[0]** and **i[1]**. **i**, a three-dimensional array and its two elements, each of which are two-dimensional arrays, are graphically represented in Figure 1.40.

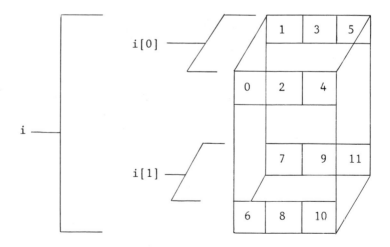

Figure 1.40 Graphical representation of a three dimensional array

Similarly, the definition defines six other one dimensional arrays: **i[0][0], i[0][1], i[0][2], i[1][0], i[1][1]**, and **i[1][2]**. The first three compose the elements of the array **i[0]**, and the remaining three compose the elements of the array **i[1]**. **i[0]** and its elements are graphically represented in Figure 1.41.

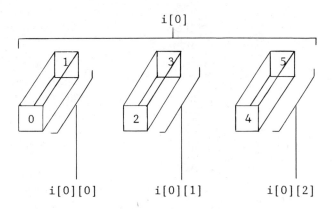

Figure 1.41 Decomposition of an array element that is itself an array

Finally, the one-dimensional array **i[0][0]** consists of two elements **i[0][0][0]** and **i[0][0][1]** that are integers initialized to the values 0 and 1 respectively. More generally, the base-element type of an array may be a structure, union, fundamental data object, or another type array.

If an array is not explicitly dimensioned in a definition, its dimensions must be deducible from an initialization accompanying its definition. The instances in which an array dimension is considered unnecessary are when it is the left-most dimension in a declaration for a:

1.   formal parameter

2.   external object

If an array only has one dimension, then that dimension is the left-most dimension.

Array definitions indicate the maximum number of elements that are considered to be in any one array dimension. The dimension values are used by C to reserve sufficient storage at array memory allocation (definition) time. Thereafter, the values are only used in associated array-element references which are automatically converted to pointer arithmetic operations involving computations scaled by the array dimensions. The dimension values are never used as reasonability values in the subsequent, array-element reference requests. Thus, C provides no bounds-checking on array subscripts. As an immediate consequence, in many implementations, arrays can be quietly indexed out-of-bounds and surrounding data destroyed. String operations require particular vigilance since they usually involve manipulation of variable length character clumps within the fixed boundary of a character array.

Though array definitions indicate the maximum number of elements that are considered to be in any one array dimension, the individual elements are referenced using **zero origin indexing**. Thus, the first element has an index of zero and is best referred to as the **initial** or **zeroth** element.

Array elements are stored in memory in **row major** order. In this method, the last subscript varies the fastest as the elements are stored from the lowest memory address to the highest. See Figure 1.42.

```
int x[2][3][2];
```

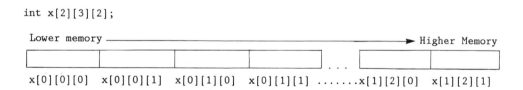

Figure 1.42 How array elements are conceptually located in memory

The Relationship Between Arrays and Pointers

Since all array indexing is converted to pointer arithmetic, a very strong relationship exists in C between arrays and pointers. In general, any indexed array expression is equivalent to a corresponding pointer and offset expression. As an example, any pointer variable can be subscripted regardless of whether or not it points to an array. Beware that if the pointer variable does not point to an array, it most likely points to trouble.

Specifically, if **pa** is a pointer to objects of type **t**, and **a** is an array of type **t**, then the following is true:

```
t   a[20];
t   *pa = &a[0];      /* point pa at a */
```

Expression	Equivalent Expression	
pa = &a[0]	pa = a	
a[n]	(*(a+n))	/* note outermost parentheses */
&a[n]	a+n	
&a[n]	&a[0] + n	
pa[n]	(*(pa+n))	/* note outermost parentheses */

Note the outermost parentheses on the second and last equivalent expression. These parentheses are generally required in the event that the expression **(*(a + n))** or **pa[n]** is followed by a second set of bracketed subscripts that would have a higher precedence than the indirection operator incorporated in the equivalent expression. These relationships are extendable to multi-dimensional arrays. Consider:

```
int b[4][5];
```

Expression	Equivalent Expression
b[n][m]	(*(b+n))[m]

In this case, the expression ***(b + n)[m]** would not be equivalent to **b[n][m]**.

In C, a definition of a multi-dimensional array results in the definition of more than one array. In Figure 1.43, nine arrays are defined with one definition.

Consider the expression **i[1][1][1]**. C resolves this with pointer arithmetic as indicated in Figure 1.44.

, 1, 2, 3, 4, 5, 6, 7, 8, 9, 10, 11 };

Array Elements

	First Element	Subsequent Elements	sizeof Elements*
i		i[1]	12
i[0]	[0]	i[0][1], i[0][2]	4
i[1]	[0]	i[1][1], i[0][2]	4
i[0][0]	[0][0]	i[0][0][1]	2
i[0][1]	[1][0]	i[0][1][1]	2
i[0][2]	[2][0]	i[0][2][1]	2
i[1][0]	[0][0]	i[1][0][1]	2
i[1][1]	[1][0]	i[1][1][1]	2
i[1][2]	[2][0]	i[1][2][1]	2

* sizeof(pointers) == 2

Figure 1.43 Nine arrays and their elements created by one definition

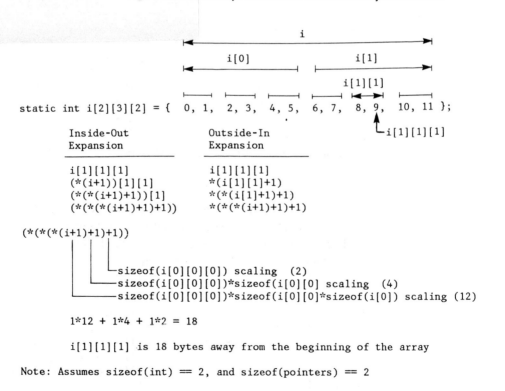

```
Inside-Out                Outside-In
Expansion                 Expansion

i[1][1][1]                i[1][1][1]
(*(i+1))[1][1]            *(i[1][1]+1)
(*(*(i+1)+1))[1]          *(*(i[1]+1)+1)
(*(*(*(i+1)+1)+1))        *(*(*(i+1)+1)+1)
```

```
(*(*(*(i+1)+1)+1))
```
```
       sizeof(i[0][0][0]) scaling  (2)
     sizeof(i[0][0][0])*sizeof(i[0][0] scaling  (4)
   sizeof(i[0][0][0])*sizeof(i[0][0]*sizeof(i[0]) scaling (12)
```

1*12 + 1*4 + 1*2 = 18

i[1][1][1] is 18 bytes away from the beginning of the array

Note: Assumes sizeof(int) == 2, and sizeof(pointers) == 2

Figure 1.44 Resolution of array indexes via pointer arithmetic

Note that in Figure 1.43 the **sizeof(i)** is not needed in the pointer arithmetic calculation. This is why the left-most dimension is never needed when declaring external arrays or dimensions of formal parameter arrays.

Whenever an array name is used in any expression except as an argument to **sizeof**, the array name and accompanying information is converted to a pointer using pointer arithmetic involving scaling. For example, consider the definitions:

```
int a[3]    = { 0, 1, 2 };
int b[3][2] = { 0, 1, 2, 3, 4, 5 };
```

None of the following expressions has enough information to select a unique integer: **a, b, b[1]**. The expressions therefore are converted to pointers that point at the items listed in Figure 1.45.

Expression	Points At
a	a[0]
b	b[0]
b[1]	b[1][0]

Figure 1.45 Pointer expressions and their targets

More generally, such expressions are the names of arrays that are converted to pointers that point at their first element. The relationship is important because, if you consider the definition in Figure 1.44, it is clear that:

Expression	Points at	Summarized Relationship		
i	i[0]	i ⟶ i[0] ⟶ i[0][0] ⟶ i[0][0][0]		
i[0]	i[0][0]		i[0][1] ⟶ i[0][1][0]	
i[1]	i[1][0]		i[0][2] ⟶ i[0][2][0]	
i[0][0]	i[0][0][0]	i[1] ⟶ i[1][0] ⟶ i[1][0][0]		
			i[1][1] ⟶ i[1][1][0]	
			i[1][2] ⟶ i[1][2][0]	

It is commonly written that an array name is converted to a pointer that points at its initial element. The above discussion clearly indicates that the initial element is not necessarily the initial base element of the array. Therefore, the following is true:

```
static int i[2][3][2] = { 0, 1, 2, 3, 4, 5, 6, 7, 8, 9, 10, 11 };
```

expression	sizeof expression*	first equivalent expression	second equivalent expression	points at
i	24	n/a	n/a	i[0]
i[0]	12	(*(i+0))	*i	i[0][0]
i[0][0]	4	(*(*(i+0)+0))	**i	i[0][0][0]
i[0][0][0]	2	(*(*(*(i+0)+0)+0))	***i	n/a

```
*assumes sizeof(int) == 2 is true
```

The relationship becomes confusing when one realizes that the pointers generated by the expressions **i, i[0],** and **i[0][0]** all have the same value. If any one of them were indiscreetly used as an assignment value to a pointer **p** declared to point to **int**s, then **p** would point to **i[0][0][0]** and the multiple levels of indirection **i** is required to traverse would not be required for **p**. But, as is indicated by the **sizeof** calculations in the process of expression evaluation, the expressions are very different to the compiler.

The generated pointers are not pointer variables, therefore, expressions such as **i ++, i[0] ++** and **i[0][0]** are illegal, just as 75 ++ would be illegal. In other words, the expressions are not **lvalues**, they are **rvalues**. However, even this situation becomes hazy when such expressions are included in function calls as in Figure 1.46.

In **calling_fun**, attempted use of the expression **int_array ++** would be illegal. Yet, when the pointer generated by the expression **int_array** is passed to **called_fun** and assigned to the formal parameter **array**, the expression **array ++** is permitted. Because **array** is a formal parameter, it is treated differently than an automatic array would be.

That is, in Figure 1.47, both **argv1** and **argv2** are pointer variables that point to arrays, but they must be declared differently because one is a formal parameter while the other is not.

```
                              int a;

   calling_fun                called_fun(array)
   {                          /* sizeof(array) == sizeof(int *) */
         int int_array[20];   int array[];
          . . . .            {
                                . . . . .
       called_fun(int_array);    a = *(array++);
          . . . .                . . . . .
   }                          }
```

Figure 1.46 "Passing" arrays in function calls

```
   char *argv1[];
{
   char *(*argv2)[50]; /* argv1 and argv2 have similar properties */
          . . . . .
   argv2 = argv1;          /* ...so set them equal...                 */

}
```

Figure 1.47 Formal parameter array and automatic variable equivalent

In summary, there is no such thing as a formal parameter array because arrays cannot be passed except when they are members of a structure. Therefore, the fact that **array** is declared as an array is recognized and accommodated accordingly by the compiler. It is treated differently than an automatic or directly referenced external array.

Note that the array size is missing since it is the left-most (and only) array dimension that is needed only for storage allocation and not for pointer arithmetic scaling. The declaration could be, and actually is, replaced with the equivalent declaration:

```
        int *array;
```

This would perhaps make more sense when used with the expression:

```
        a = *(array++);
```

These notions are often applied in accessing the command line parameters within a C program. At entry, **main( )** can be declared as:

```
main(argc,argv)              main(argc,argv)
int argc;          - or -    int argc;
char *argv[];                char **argv;
```

The program entry passed parameter structure is illustrated in Figure 1.48.

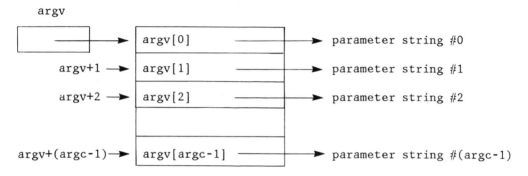

Figure 1.48 Relationship of argc and argv

In C, expressions such as:

```
*argv[i]    and    **(argv+i)
```

are equivalent by definition. Using such arrays of pointers to character strings of different length can result in a storage savings. Otherwise, array storage of unequal length character strings would force storage allocation for each string equal to the length of the longest string.

Structures

Structures are objects that, like arrays, are composed of other objects. The objects that comprise a structure are fundamental data type objects, arrays, pointers, unions, and other types of structures. A structure can never contain an instance of itself, though it can contain an instance of a pointer to itself. Compilers adhering to the X3J11 standard allow different structures to have members of the same name without conflict. That is, member names and their types are local to their structures.

Structures and arrays are different in the following ways:

1. The objects that comprise a structure are possibly of different types. The objects that comprise an array are always of the same type.

2. The objects that comprise a structure are referred to as **members** instead of as **elements**.

3. The compiler does not convert the name of a structure to a pointer as it does with an array.

Structure Declarations and Definitions

An example of structure declaration, sometimes referred to as a **structure template**, is indicated in Figure 1.49. Like fundamental data types, the scope of a structure declaration depends on where it is defined.

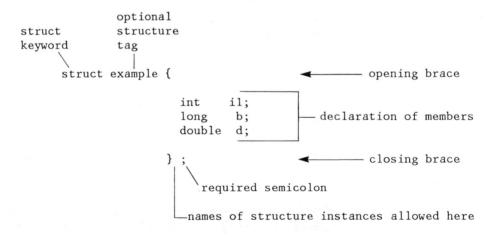

Figure 1.49 General format of a structure declaration

Once declared, the **structure-tag** can then be used in other definitions and declarations as indicated in Figure 1.50. When an instance of a structure is defined, it is referred to as a **structure variable**.

```
struct example examp, *examp_ptr=&examp, examp_array[10];
typedef struct examp EXAMP_STRUCT, *EXAMP_STRUCT_PTR;
```

Figure 1.50 Defining objects using an existing structure declaration

The only valid operators that can be applied to a structure variable are the **sizeof**, **&**, and **member selection** operators. Structure variables may not be used in logical equality testing and assignment operations though they may be passed to and returned by functions with X3J11.

Note that the definitions in Figure 1.50 define a structure, a structure pointer, and an array of structures.

Alternately, structure instances may accompany the structure declaration as in Figure 1.51.

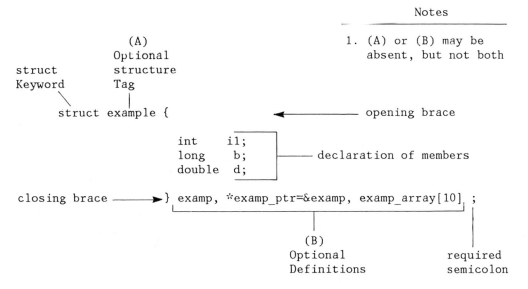

Figure 1.51 Example of structure declaration and structure variable definition

Including optional definitions with a structure declaration is allowed but not generally recommended. Such declarations cannot be part of a header file that is included more than once in a program because of the resulting redefinition of the structure variables.

Structure Member Selection

To select the integer member **il** in the struct **examp**, you would use the member selection operator as indicated in Figure 1.52.

```
int i;

        i =  examp.il  /* selects the correct member */
```

Figure 1.52 Selecting a member within a structure variable

Noting that **examp__ptr** was declared to be a pointer to structures of type **example** and was initialized to point to the structure variable **examp**, we can also write:

```
i =  (*examp_ptr).il;  /* selects the correct member */

                - or -

i =  examp_ptr -> il;  /* selects the correct member */
```

Note that the parentheses are required in the first version because the precedence of the member selection operator is higher than the indirection operator. Regardless of the version used, once a member is selected the selecting expression possesses all the data attributes of the selected member. For example, if a member is a pointer, then all valid operations involving pointers may be applied to an expression that selects that member. Figure 1.53 shows a structure and structure pointer example.

The relationships are illustrated graphically in Figure 1.54.

Structure Equality

Two structures are considered equal when they are declared to be of the same type and each of their corresponding members has the same value. However, because members within the same structure may be of different types, they may have varying memory alignment requirements, resulting in "holes" within the structure (between members) and padding at the end of a structure (to facilitate manipulation of arrays of structures.) As a direct consequence, though two structures may be equal, if

```
struct struct2 {
                int i1;
                float f1;
          } s2;

struct struct1 {                          ?
                int i4;
                struct *struct2 struct2_ptr;
          } s1, *s1_ptr = &s1;

     s1.struct2_ptr = &s2;      /* point pointer at s2 */
```

Expression	Comment
s1_ptr	points at s1
(*s1_ptr)	equivalent to s1
s1_ptr->	equivalent to s1
(*s1_ptr).struct2_ptr	equiv. to s1.struct2_ptr, points at s2
s1_ptr->struct2_ptr	equiv. to s1->struct2_ptr, points at s2
(*(*s1_ptr).struct2_ptr)	equivalent to s2
(*(s1_ptr->struct2_ptr))	equivalent to s2
(*(*s1_ptr).struct2_ptr).f1	equivalent to s2.f1
((*s1_ptr).struct2_ptr)->f1	equivalent to s2.f1
(*(s1_ptr->struct2_ptr)).f1	equivalent to s2.f1
(s1_ptr->struct2_ptr)->f1	equivalent to s2.f1

Figure 1.53 Structure and structure pointer example

the structures are compared on a byte-for-byte basis, they will often differ because the irrelevant values within the holes and/or padding are unequal.

The X3J11 standard allows structure assignments via the = assignment operator. Prior to X3J11, to set one structure equal to another, one had to set each individual element in the target equal to its corresponding counterpart member in the source array via individual assignment operations. Alternately, one could have used a block-memory move to copy the source structure to the target structure. For obvious reasons, the copying had to be done as a block-memory move operation, not a string operation.

Finally, because machine architectures have varying alignment requirements, structure data written on one machine may

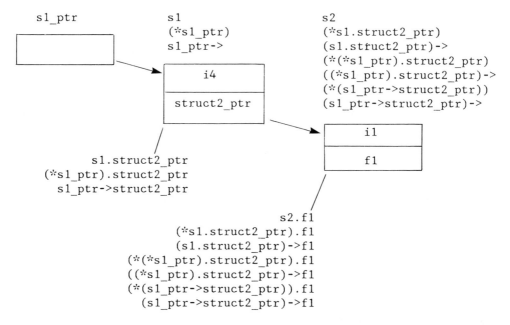

Figure 1.54 Pictorial relationship of Figure 1.53 declaration/definitions

not be usable on another. Again, this is due to the varying hole and padding patterns resulting from varying object alignment requirements. It is even conceivable that two different compilers for a given machine have assumed different alignments for objects, resulting in data that are not readable for programs compiled on the same machine but by another compiler.

Passing and Returning Structures

Compilers adhering to the X3J11 standard allow functions to pass/return structures to/from other functions. When a structure is passed, the receiving function obtains an image of the original structure and has no access to the original structure; this is a strict call by value. When a structure pointer is passed, the called function has complete access to the original structure.

Passing a structure containing an array as its only member provides a mechanism for array passing between functions.

Hazard:

It is easy to pass a structure to a function when it is expecting a pointer to a structure and vice versa.

```
int lat;

struct position {
                float latitude;
                float longitude;
              };

struct city {
              char name[30];
              struct position };

struct city capitol[50];

            lat =  capitol[0].position.latitude;
```

Figure 1.55 An example of using an array whose elements are nested structures

Arrays of Structures

As indicated in Figure 1.51, C permits arrays whose elements are structures. Access to individual array element structures is illustrated in Figure 1.55.

Nested Structures

Structures may be nested, though occurrences of a given structure cannot occur, either directly or indirectly, within themselves. This means that mutually recursive structures are strictly prohibited. Instances of pointers to a given type structure are allowed within the given type structure. The rules of member selection are illustrated in Figure 1.55.

Bit Fields

A bit field is a set of contiguous bits within a word that is treated as an integer. Bit fields allow the creation of variables that occupy one or more bits of storage, though they can never occupy more bits than are contained in a machine word. With some compilers, bit fields are always treated as unsigned variables. X3J11 allows both signed and unsigned bit fields.

Almost everything having to do with bit fields is implementation-dependent. In some cases, overflow of bit-field values can affect storage of nearby structure members.

Hazard:

Avoid bit fields wherever possible.

Generally, the compiler places adjacent bit-field definitions within a machine's storage word until there is not sufficient room for the next bit field. Then, the next word is used for the next bit field. C does not permit a bit field to span words.

The direction of placement of bit fields within a word, right-to-left or left-to-right, is not specified by C. In addition, since word sizes vary between machines, bit-field data are extremely machine- and implementation-sensitive and are therefore largely unportable if they are communicated to the outside world as bit-field data. Bit fields can also be used safely as private, internal program indicators that are never externally visible.

Bit fields are members of structures. An example of defining bit-field variables is provided in Figure 1.56.

```
struct bit_field_struct {
    long l1;       /* can mix bit fields with non bit field members */
    unsigned field1:6;   /* field1 is six bits wide           */
    unsigned field2:1;   /* field2 is one bit  wide           */
    unsigned       :3;   /* unnamed ==> reserves three bits */
    unsigned field3:2;   /* field3 is two bits wide           */
    unsigned       :0;   /* forces alignment to next word   */
    unsigned field4:4;   /* field4 is four bits wide           */
    short s1;      /* can mix bit fields with non bit field members */
};
```

Figure 1.56 Declaring a structure with bit fields

Unnamed bit fields reserve storage unless their length is zero, in which case the next bit field, if any, is aligned on the next word boundary. A bit field cannot span a word. If it does not fit within the current target word, it is aligned on the next word boundary. Because bit fields are not necessarily aligned on a character boundary, the address operator **&** cannot be applied to them. Finally, C does not allow arrays of bit fields.

To select a bit field member of a **struct**, the normal member selection rules apply as indicated in Figure 1.57.

```
int i;
struct bit_field_struct bfs;

    bfs.field1 = 22;      /* field1 is six bits wide */
        . . . . . . .

    i = bfs.field1/4;     /* field1 is six bits wide */
```

Figure 1.57 Accessing bit field variables

Unions

Unions are similar to structures. Compilers implement unions so that individual members all have zero displacement from the beginning of the structure and therefore share common memory. This is a requirement with X3J11. Beware that union members can overlap any way the compiler wishes.

Hazard:

While union members have zero displacement from the beginning of a union, make no assumption regarding the overlapping of union members.

The **sizeof** a union is the amount of memory it occupies plus any padding to facilitate array processing. This can be the **sizeof** its largest member, though it need not be. Like structures, individual objects are distinguished from one another by unique member names and are selected by using the **.** (dot) operator. With X3J11, member names are local to structures.

Hazard:

It is the programmer's responsibility to keep track of the contents of a union.

All of the normal member selection and declaration of structures apply as indicated in Figures 1.58 and 1.59.

As with structures, the only valid operators that can be applied to a union are the address operator (**&**), member selection operator (**.**), and **sizeof** operator.

```
union example {
        int     i;              /* occupies bytes 0 through 1 */
        float   f;              /* occupies bytes 0 through 3 */
        double d;               /* occupies bytes 0 through 7 */
        char    c[10];          /* occupies bytes 0 through 9 */
        };
```

Figure 1.58 Declaration of a union

```
int     i2;
float   f2;
union example exampl;
                    .   .   .   .   .
```

```
        exampl.i = i2 = 25;         /* exampl union has an integer  */
        f2 = exampl.f = 226.442;    /* exampl union now has a float */
```

Figure 1.59 Accessing a union member

Initialization

Variables can be initialized only at their point of definition (storage allocation point). This means **extern** storage class variables usually cannot be initialized where they are declared as **extern** variables.

All **static** storage class variables, whether scalar or aggregate, are initialized to zero if they are not initialized at their point of definition. Scalar variables occupying **static** storage can be initialized only with constant expressions.

All **auto** and **register** storage class variables, whether scalar or aggregate, are guaranteed to contain random values if they are not explicitly initialized at their point of definition. Scalar **auto** and **register** storage class variables can be initialized via an assignment with any valid expression that optionally involves any known variable. Such an initialization is equivalent to a variable declaration followed immediately by an ordinary assignment statement.

All scalar variables can be initialized when defined. If the storage class of the scalar is **static**, then the initialization occurs only once— conceptually by the compiler. In the case of **auto** and **register** storage class scalar variables, the initialization assignment occurs at each entry to the owning block.

scalar variables

Figure 1.60 shows the initializing of scalar variables.

```
int     i = 25 + 65;  /* constant expression, valid everywhere */
float   f = 226.42;   /* constant expression, valid everywhere */
char    c = 'a';      /* constant expression, valid everywhere */
long    l = -336/i;   /* valid only for auto or register storage class */
double  d = f*224.32; /* valid only for auto storage class */
```

Figure 1.60 Initializing scalar variables

pointers

Initializing pointers at their definition requires caution. The first example in Figure 1.61 shows a pointer being initialized to 5 when the intent was probably to initialize the object it points at to 5. Assigning 5 to a target object would occur if the pointer were pointing at a valid object when the statement:

```
*flt_ptr1 = 5;     /* *flt_ptr gets 5 */
```

was subsequently encountered.

A definition such as:

```
float *flt_ptr, *fp = 5;
```

is still incorrect.

The second example in Figure 1.61 illustrates how to initialize an array pointer. Note that the second example is allowed anywhere.

```
float *flt_ptr = 5;      /* DANGER !! flt_ptr gets 5, NOT *flt_ptr   */
char *ptr = "bacacac";   /* allowed as automatic variable            */
float *flt_ptr2 = &fl;   /* only allowed as an automatic variable    */
```

Figure 1.61 Initializing pointers

arrays

Prior to X3J11, automatic arrays could never be initialized; the array elements were guaranteed to contain random values until explicitly assigned a value. **Static** storage class character arrays could be initialized by setting them equal to a character string as in Figure 1.62. Note that this is an initialization and not an assignment operation despite the fact that the = operator is used.

```
char  msg[]    = "Hello";
char  msg[]    = { 'H', 'e', 'l', 'l', 'o', '\0' };
```

Figure 1.62 Initializing a static storage class character array with a string and an equivalent initialization using individual characters

The dimensions of an array can be implicitly determined by its initializer. In Figure 1.62, the array **msg** has a rank of six. If the number of explicit initializers is fewer than the number of array elements, the uninitialized elements are automatically set to zero. If the number of explicit initializers is greater than the number of array elements, then the initialization is flagged as an error by the compiler.

There are several ways to initialize an array. Figure 1.63 illustrates some of them.

```
int array[2][3] = {   0, 1, 2,     3, 0, 0 };
int array[2][3] = { { 0, 1, 2 }, { 3, 0, 0 } };
int array[2][3] = { { 0, 1, 2 }, { 3 } };
```

Figure 1.63 Equivalent array initialization

Finally, it is useful to create arrays of pointers to strings. Such constructs conserve storage and are discussed in the discussion of Figure 1.48. Figure 1.64 shows how to achieve this.

```
char *msgs[] = { "This is message zero",
                 "This is message one",
                 "This is message two",
               };
```

Figure 1.64 Initializing an array of pointers to strings

structures

With X3J11, structures can always be initialized regardless of storage class. With **auto** storage class structures, individual members are guaranteed to contain random values until they are explicitly assigned a value. Uninitialized **static** storage class members are guaranteed to contain zeros. Figure 1.65 shows equivalent ways to initialize structures.

Arrays of structures can also be initialized as indicated in Figure 1.66.

The initialization of structures within structures is shown in Figure 1.67.

unions

With X3J11, unions can always be initialized regardless of storage class.

```
struct example { char *msg_ptr;
                 int  i1;
                 char msg[20];
               } exampl = { "Hello", 52, "This is a message"}, examp2;

                        -or-

struct example { char *msg_ptr;
                 int  i1;
                 char msg[20];
               };
struct example exampl = { "Hello", 52, "This is a message"}, examp2;
```

Figure 1.65 Equivalent initialization of static storage structures

```
struct example { char *msg_ptr;
                 int  i1;
                 char msg[20];
               };

struct example exampl[3] = { { "Hello1", 52, "This is message zero" },
                             { "Hello2", 99, "This is message one" }, };
```

Figure 1.66 Initialization of an array of static storage structures

```
#include "stdio.h"

main()
{
   struct type1 { int i; float f; };
   struct type2 { char msg[20]; struct type1 x; };

   static struct type2 example = { {"hello there"} , { 999, 2.256 } };

   printf("example.msg = %s, example.x.i = %d, example.x.f = %f",\
          example.msg,      example.x.i,      example.x.f);
}
```

Figure 1.67 Initialization of structures within structures

C Operators

- **Primary Expression Operators**
- **Unary Operators**
- **Binary Operators**

Operators are applied to operands to produce a value. Like all C tokens, operators may be surrounded by white space to increase readability. However, some operators require surrounding white space. Consider the statement

```
a = b/*c; /* subtle error - a gets b every time !  */
```

What should be a division of **b** by the object pointed to by **c** is interpreted as the variable **b** immediately adjacent to the opening of a comment. This occurs because there is no space or parentheses between the division operator and the indirection operator.

Before discussing the various operators in their order of precedence, note that the operators $\sim$, $<<$, $>>$, $\&$, $:$, $\hat{}$, $\& =$, $: =$, $\hat{} =$, $<< =$, and $>> =$ have varying degrees of precedence though they share the common notion of bit manipulation. Moreover, some operators require integer operands.

Finally, the precedence of operators can be overridden by using parentheses. In this case, the evaluation commences at the deepest level of parenthesis and progresses outward. However, expressions that exist at a given level can be evaluated in any order. Compilers can also rearrange operands of commutative operators even in the presence of enclosing parentheses that would seem to indicate a different order.

Figure 2.1 is a summary chart of operators and their precedence.

Primary Expression Operators

Primary expression operators are operators that are applied to primary expressions such as identifiers, strings, constants, etc. They associate from left to right.

Expressions in parentheses are primary expressions also.

Function Call ( )

When a primary expression of type **function returning** is followed by the function call operator that contains zero or more expressions separated by commas, the corresponding function is invoked and the enclosed arguments are passed by

class	operator name	operator	direction	precedence
Primary Expression	Function call Array element Struct pointer Struct member	() [] -> . defined	⟶	1	HIGH
Unary	Auto-PostIncrement Auto-PostDecrement	++ --	⟶	
Unary	Logical negation Ones complement Arithmetic Negation Unary Plus Pointer Auto-PreIncrement Auto-PreDecrement Address Cast	! ~ - + * ++ -- & (type) sizeof	⟵	2
Multiplicative	Multiplication Division Modulus	* / %	⟶	3
Additive		+ -	⟶	4
Bitwise Shift	Shift left Shift right	<< >>	⟶	5
Relational		< <= > >=	⟶	6
Equality		== !=	⟶	7
Bitwise	AND	&	⟶	8
Bitwise	Exclusive OR	^	⟶	9
Bitwise	Inclusive OR	|	⟶	10
Logical	Logical AND	&&	⟶	11
Logical	Logical OR	||	⟶	12
Ternary	Conditional	? :	⟵	13
Assignment	 Shift Bitwise Bitwise	= %= += -= *= /= >>= <<= &= ~= |=	⟵	14
	comma	,	⟶	15	LOW

Figure 2.1 Summary chart of operators and their precedence

value. Note that the function call operator should not be confused with the parentheses separators used, for example, in arithmetic expressions.

Subscript [ ]

When a primary expression of type **array of type** is followed by one or more subscript operators containing integer expressions, the corresponding pointer arithmetic is invoked to produce the appropriate object.

Note that **a[b]** is always exactly equivalent to **(*(a + b))**.

Struct/Union Pointer – >

When a primary expression of type **pointer to struct** or **pointer to union** is followed by the struct pointer operator, which is in turn followed by a member of the type structure or union, a corresponding instance of the structure/union variable is produced.

The struct pointer operator can be preceded by an integer constant that is cast to a valid type as indicated in Figure 2.2. In this case, the integer value points at a memory address. The portability of this technique is nonexistent.

Note that **a –> b** is equivalent to **(*a).b**. Moreover, since ***a** is always an **lvalue**, **a –>** is always an **lvalue** .

```
pop = ((struct city_ptr) 0x2F34) -> population;  /* non-portable */
```

Figure 2.2 Using a pointer derived by casting a constant

Struct/Union Member (Dot Operator) .

When a primary expression of type **struct** or **union** is followed by the struct member operator, which is in turn followed by a member of the type structure or union, a corresponding instance of the structure/union member is produced.

The **.** operator yields an **lvalue** if its left operand is an **lvalue**.

Unary Operators

Unary operators require only one operand. They associate right to left. Note that some binary operators such as **.** and −> bind more tightly than the Unary operators.

Logical Negation !

The logical negation operator requires a scalar type operand and returns an **int**. If the operand is non-zero (TRUE), then the result is zero (FALSE). If the operand is zero (FALSE), then the result is 1 (TRUE). As a direct consequence, the following is true for all valid objects **x**:

$$(\ (!x) \ == \ (x{==}0) \ )$$

The logical negation, bitwise negation, and unary minus operators are often confused. Figure 2.3 provides a summary comparison table for reference and assumes a two's complement machine in the interpretation of the bitwise negation results.

Also, see the sections titled *Bitwise Negation* and *Unary Minus Operators*.

Unary Operator		Operand		
		-1	0	1
logical negation	(!)	0	1	0
bitwise negation	(~)	0	-1	-2
unary minus	(-)	1	0	-1

Figure 2.3 Logical negation vs. bitwise negation vs. unary minus

Bitwise Negation (Ones' Complement) ~

The bitwise negation operator requires an integral type operand. It produces a ones' complement value of the operand. As such the following relationship is always true for two's complement machines:

$$(\sim x \ == \ -(x{+}1))$$

The bitwise negation operator facilitates portability of expressions involving different size **int**s on different machines by avoiding hard-coded constants in bit manipulation expressions. In the following example the first expression works correctly and independently of the machine's **int** size. The second does not, potentially zeroing the highorder bits on machines of longer **int** length.

```
val = i & (~0x3F);    /* GOOD - sizeof(int) insensitive */
val = i & (0xFFC0);   /* BAD  - sizeof(int)   sensitive */
```

Also, see the sections titled *Logical Negation* and *Unary Minus Operators*.

Unary Minus (Arithmetic Negation) −

The unary minus operator requires an integral type operand. It produces an arithmetic (two's complement) of an **int** type operand.

Also, see the sections titled *Logical Negation* and *Bitwise Negation Operators*.

Unary Plus +

The unary plus operator requires an integral type operand. In X3J11, this operator forces the compiler to evaluate the expression as written. Otherwise, it has no effect.

Indirection (Pointer) *

The indirection operator allows the referencing of an object via a pointer (indirection.) If **a** is an object, then it is always true that:

$$(*(\&a) == a)$$

Similarly,

```
type *ptr, x, a;        ptr = &a, x = *ptr;

            - is equivalent to -

type  x, a;       x = a;
```

Also, if **ptr** is a pointer to an arithmetic object, then:

```
*ptr + 1
```

produces an incremented value of the object while

```
*(p+1)
```

produces the value of an adjacent object of similar type.

Do not confuse the indirection operator with the multiplicative operator. Also, see the sections titled *Pointer Arithmetic* and the *Address Operator*.

Auto-Increment + +

The auto-increment operators require arithmetic lvalues as operands. Because C does not guarantee the order of evaluation of expressions, use temporary variables to avoid multiple instances of operands in a single statement that are subject to one or more applications of an auto-increment operator. See the following example:

```
a[i++][j++] = i+j;   /* NON-PORTABLE AND UNPREDICTABLE */

                  - vs. -

i1 = i++, j1 = j++, a[i1][j1] = i+j;   /* portable and predictable */
```

Pre-Increment

The pre-increment version of the auto-increment operator produces an incremented value of the object that replaces the original value during the evaluation of the expression in the following example:

```
val = 5;
i = ++val;    /* i gets 6 , val gets 6 */
```

Post-Increment

The post-increment version of the auto-increment operator produces the current value of an object, which is replaced by an incremented value during the evaluation of the expression. The actual incrementing of the operand can be deferred until the next semicolon as shown in the following example:

```
val = 5;
i = val++;    /* i gets 5 , val gets 6 */
```

Note that $(++x)$ is equivalent to $(x +=1)$, but $(++x)$ has higher precedence. Both expressions differ from the expression $(x = x + 1)$ because they may only require one memory reference while the latter may require two, depending on the implementation.

Auto-Decrement

The auto-decrement operators require arithmetic lvalues as operands. Because C does not guarantee the order of evaluation of expressions, use temporary variables to avoid multiple instances of operands in a single statement, which are subject to one or more applications of an auto-decrement operator as in the following example:

```
a[i--][j--] = i+j;   /* NON-PORTABLE AND UNPREDICTABLE */

                  - vs. -

i1 = i--, j1 = j--, a[i1][j1] = i+j;   /* portable and predictable */
```

Pre-Decrement

The pre-decrement version of the auto-decrement operator produces a decremented value of the object, which replaces the original value during the evaluation of the expression as shown in the following example:

```
val = 5;
i = --val;   /* i gets 4 , val gets 4 */
```

Post-Decrement

The post-decrement version of the auto-decrement operator produces the current value of an object, which is replaced by a decremented value during the evaluation of the expression as shown in the following example:

```
val = 5;
i = val--;   /* i gets 5 , val gets 4 */
```

Address &

The address operator produces a pointer of type **t*** when applied to an object of type **t**. Because of typing and automatic promotion considerations, the address operator generally cannot be applied to formal parameters without compiler implementation hazards.

Cast (type)

The cast operator evaluates the expression following the casting parentheses and converts the resulting value to the format/-representation specified in the casting parentheses. The cast operator cannot be applied to functions or arrays and should not be applied to pointers except for returned memory allocation pointer values. The cast operator is useful for coercing returned and passed values to correct representations. A complex example using the cast operator is shown in Figure 2.4.

The creation and unraveling of casting specifications is similar to corresponding **typedef** procedures, except that no synonym is specified.

Also, see *Understanding and Creating Object Declarations* and *typedef -Derived Data Typing*.

```
long *long_ptr;

struct city { char name[30];
             int latitude, longitude, population;
           };

typedef struct city  CAPITOL, *CAPITOL_PTR, **PTR_TO_CITY_PTRS;

struct city *((*ptr_2_array_of_ptrs)[10]);

    long_ptr = ( long *) calloc( 1, sizeof(long) );

ptr_2_array_of_ptrs=(struct city *((*)[10])) calloc(1,sizeof((CAPITOL **)));

                          -or-

ptr_2_array_of_ptrs=(CAPITOL_PTR((*)[10])) calloc(1,sizeof(PTR_TO_CITY_PTRS));
```

Figure 2.4 Complex example using the cast operator

sizeof

The **sizeof** operator provides the width of an operand in terms of **char** (byte) units. Note that the operand of the **sizeof** operator is not evaluated, it is simply parsed to obtain its type. Thus, the statement:

```
s = sizeof(x++);
```

leaves **x** unincremented.

When applied to a character array initialized without a dimension via a string constant, the value produced includes the terminating null. This value will be one unit larger than would be indicated by the **strlen** function.

The **sizeof** operator has two forms, one for object types and one for expressions as shown in Figure 2.5. The object-type variant requires parentheses around the type. The parentheses are optional for an expression operand.

Note that for an array **x**, using **x** in the context of **sizeof(x)** results in **x** being considered as an array and not as a pointer to the first element of **x**.

```
double *dbl_ptr;

        sizeof(  long[50] )     /* object type variant */
        sizeof( *long[50] )     /* object type variant */

        sizeof(*dbl_ptr)        /* expression type variant */
        sizeof *dbl_ptr         /* expression type variant */
```

Figure 2.5 The two forms of the sizeof operator

Binary Operators

Binary operators require two operands.

Multiplicative Operators

Multiplicative Operators are the normal operators associated with scalar objects. In the case of **int** multiplication and division, overflow and underflow situations will not be reported during program execution.

Multiplication *

In the example Figure 2.21, the order of evaluation within the parentheses is not specified. This may introduce overflow and underflow errors for signed calculations (overflow and underflow do not happen with unsigned objects) depending on the compiler. Whether such errors are reported is implementation-dependent.

```
val = (a*b*c);
```

Nested parentheses do not solve the problem either, so it is best to use intermediate variables to force the evaluation order, as follows:

Hazard:

The multiplication operator and the unary indirection operator are easily confused. Consider the plight of the hapless FORTRAN programmer who codes the following:

```
a = b**c;
```

expecting to achieve exponentiation.

Division /

The division operator discards any remainder in integer division even if the resulting value is immediately assigned or cast to a **double** or **float** object. If the result is negative, the direction of truncation is unspecified.

Modulus %

The modulus operator requires **int** operands. It produces the integer remainder computed by dividing the first operand by the second, as shown in the following example:

```
((1015 % 100) == 15)   ((27 % 4 ) == 3)   ((5 % 2) == 1) ((18 % 9 ) == 0)

      val =   ((i1 = 26) % (i2 = 3));   /* val gets 2 */+
```

It is always true that:

```
i1 = (i1/i2)*i2 + (i1%i2);
```

The importance of this identity is that, while both the direction of division truncation and the sign of the result of the % (modulus) operator are sometimes undefined, the two cannot be chosen independently. Either the remainder has the sign of the dividend and truncation is toward zero, or the remainder has the sign of the divisor and truncation is toward the next lower integer (in the direction of negative infinity).

Additive Operators

Additive operators are the normal operators that can be associated with scalar objects. These operators can be applied to pointers, in which case pointer arithmetic (scaling) occurs.

In the example shown below, the order of evaluation within the parentheses is not specified. This may introduce overflow and underflow errors for signed calculations (overflow and underflow do not happen with unsigned objects) depending on the compiler. Whether such errors are reported is implementation-dependent. Nested parentheses do not solve the problem either, so it is best to use intermediate variables to force the evaluation order, as follows:

```
val = (a+b+c);
```

Also, see *Pointer Arithmetic*.

Subtraction –

The subtraction operator is used to produce the arithmetic difference of two scalar operands. Moreover, used with pointers, it is used to point to a preceding instance of an appropriate object or to subtract two pointers, yielding the distance (in terms of elements) between two elements of the same array.

Also, see *Pointer Arithmetic*.

Addition +

The addition operator is used to produce the arithmetic sum of two scalar operands. Moreover, if one operand is a pointer, it is used to point to a subsequent instance of an appropriate object. Two pointers cannot be added.

Also, see *Pointer Arithmetic*.

Bitwise Shift Operators

The bitwise shift operators require integer operands. Do not shift an integer so far that all its bits disappear.

Bitwise Shift Left < <

The bitwise, shift-left operator shifts the first integer operand to the left the number of bits indicated by the second integer operand. The vacated bits are filled with zeros and the bits shifted out are lost, as follows:

```
val = (12 << 2 );   /* val gets 48 */
```

Bitwise Shift Right > >

The bitwise, shift-right operator shifts the first integer operand to the right the number of bits indicated by the second integer operand. The bits shifted out of the register are lost. If the first operand is positive, zero, or an **unsigned** value, the vacated bits are filled with zeros.

If the first operand is negative, the results are unpredictable but consistent in that either all ones or all zeros are shifted in. The intended result may be salvageable by using the **&** (bit-wise AND) operator to mask off possible propagated, high-order, one bits introduced by the shifting operation.

Cast all signed values to **unsigned** before shifting, as follows:

```
val = ( (il = 12) >> 2 );    /* val gets 3 */

val = ( -5 >> 2 );   /* BEWARE OF SHIFTING A NEGATIVE TO THE RIGHT */
                     /*    (( (-1) >> 1) == -1) on some machines.    */
```

Relational Operators

The relational operators allow magnitude comparison of two scalar operands. They may be used with all basic data types except **void** and cannot be applied to string constants. If the relationship is TRUE, an **int** result with a value of 1 is returned. If the relationship is FALSE, an **int** result with a value of 0 is returned. Figure 2.6 shows a summary table of the relational operators.

```
int   il = i2 = 10, i3 = 25;   /* set values for example */
```

Operator	Form	Example	Result
Less Than or Equal	<=	il <= i3	1
		il <= i2	1
Less Than	<	il < i3	1
Greater Than	>	il > i3	0
Greater Than or Equal	>=	il >= i3	0
		il >= i2	1

Figure 2.6 Summary table of the relational operators

Equality Operators

The equality operators allow comparison of two scalar operands for equality. They may be used with all basic data types except **void** and cannot be applied to string constants. If the relationship is TRUE, an **int** result with a value of 1 is returned. If the relationship is FALSE, an **int** result with a value of 0 is returned.

Hazard:

Use of these operators with floating operands is dangerous because of imprecision introduced by automatic rounding and/or truncation during expression evaluation.

Equal $==$

The equal operator tests for bit-by-bit equality. It cannot be used to test two strings for equality.

Hazard:

The simple assignment operator ($=$) is often mistakenly used in its place within conditional expressions.

Not Equal ! $=$

The not equal operator tests for inequality. Its use is illustrated in Figure 2.7.

```
int   i1 = i2 = 10, i3 = 25;   /* set values for example */
```

Operator	Form	Example	Result
Equal	==	(i1 == i3)	0
		(i1 == i2)	1
Not Equal	!=	(i1 != i3)	1
		(i1 != i2)	0

Figure 2.7 Using the Not Equal operator

Bitwise Logical Operators

The bitwise logical operators apply Boolean operations to integer operands on a bit-by-bit process.

Hazard:

Use caution with these operators in conditional expressions because the precedence of these operators is less than the precedence of the equality and relational operators, as shown in Figure 2.8.

Bitwise logical operators are subject to portability problems as a consequence of the varying size of **int**s across systems.

```
(i &  0x00FC == 0x00C0)
(i & (0x00FC == 0x00C0))
(i & (0))
(0)
```

Figure 2.8 Equivalent expressions involving haphazard use of bitwise operators

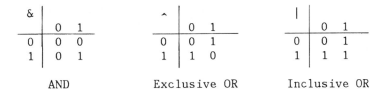

    AND   Exclusive OR   Inclusive OR

Figure 2.9 Summary table for logical bit operations

Hazard:

The bitwise logical operators are often inadvertently used in place of the intended, logical connective operators. Figure 2.10 contains a summary table comparing the effects of both the bitwise logical operators and the logical connective operators.

$2^3\ 2^2\ 2^1\ 2^0$
$8\ 4\ 2\ 1$

```
int z1 = 12, z2 = 6, z3 = 0;   /* set values for example */
```

Operator	Form	Example	Result
Bitwise AND	&	$1100\quad 0110$ (z1 & z2)	4
Bitwise Inclusive OR	|	(z1 | z2)	14
Bitwise Exclusive OR	⌐	(z1 ⌐ z2)	10
Logical AND	&&	(z1 && z2) (z1 && z3)	1 0
Logical OR	||	(z1 || z2) (z1 || z3)	1 1

Figure 2.10 Summary table of the various logical operators

AND &

The bit settings of the integer operands are ANDed to produce an **int** type value. The operation masks off selected bits and can be used with the bitwise negation operator to defeat sign extension on (signed) **char**s, and, possibly, to salvage values created by right-shifting negative values and to increase portability of code-involving bit manipulation.

Exclusive OR ⌃

The bit settings of the integer operands are exclusive ORed to produce an **int** type value. The operation toggles selected bits.

Inclusive OR |

The bit settings of the integer operands are inclusive ORed to produce an **int** type value. The operation turns on selected bits.

Logical Connective Operators

The logical connective operators are used to create compound relational tests. The operators force the order of expression evaluation within a compound relational test from left to right. Expression evaluation immediately stops when the final result can be deduced, even if the entire compound relational expression has not been entirely evaluated. For each operator, a non-zero value operand is equivalent to TRUE, while a zero value operand is equivalent to FALSE. The operand values are usually values produced by evaluating expressions involving relational operators.

Logical AND &&

The logical AND operator returns a TRUE (1) value of type **int** if both operands are TRUE (non-zero). Otherwise it returns a FALSE (0) value of type **int**.

Also, see section titled *Bitwise Logical Operators* for a comparison with the AND operator.

Logical OR ||

The logical OR operator returns a TRUE (1) value of type **int** if either operand is TRUE (non-zero). Otherwise it returns a FALSE (0) value of type **int**.

Also, see the section titled *Bitwise Logical Operators* for a comparison with the OR operator.

Conditional (Ternary) Operator ? :

The conditional operator uses three expression operands and has the format shown in Figure 2.11.

```
expression1 ? expression2 : expression3
```

Figure 2.11 Format of the conditional operator

If necessary, the type of expression2 and expression3 are promoted to the same level to avoid returning different expression types. The first expression is then evaluated. If the first expression is TRUE (non-zero), then the second expression is evaluated and its value is the value of the expression. If the first expression is FALSE (zero) then the third expression is evaluated and its value is the value of the expression. Either the second or the third expression is evaluated, but not both.

The conditional operator forces the order of evaluation within a statement and is related to the **if** statement as indicated in Figure 2.12.

```
val = ( expr1 ? expr2 : expr3 );        if ( expr1)
                                            val = expr2;
                                        else
                                            val = expr3;
```

Figure 2.12 The relationship of the if statement and conditional operator

Finally, the following oblique and, therefore, hazardous expression:

```
expr1 ? expr2 : expr3 ? expr4 : expr5
```

is equivalent to:

```
expr1 ? expr2 : (expr3 ? expr4 : expr5)
```

Assignment Operators = and ?=

Assignment operators provide one means to set an lvalue to a desired value. The first way to achieve this is through assignment via the simple = operator. However, note that the only constant that can be assigned to a pointer without being cast to the appropriate pointer type is zero.

The simple assignment operator is often inadvertently used in place of the equality operator (= =) within what should be conditional expressions (not the assignment expression resulting from the incorrect use of the assignment operator).

There are ten other operators which are summarized in Figure 2.13. Each has a binary operator counterpart, which operates at varying levels of higher precedence.

The application of these ten operators is in expressions of the form:

```
expr1 (operator)= expr2
```

This form of expression is similar to, but not identical with, an expression of the form:

```
expr1 = expr1 (operator) (expr2) /* note the parentheses around expr2 */
```

The parenthesis around **expr2** emphasize that the statement:

```
x *=  a + b;
```

is evaluated as:

```
x = x * (a + b);
```

and not as:

```
x = x * a + b;
```

The principal advantage in using these operators is that an expression such as:

```
employee[i++].salary   +=   bonus[j++]
```

is portable, while one such as:

```
employee[i++].salary = employee[i++].salary + bonus[j++]
```

is not portable because it has unpredictable side effects across C compiler implementations. The two types of expressions will never be equivalent no matter what the implementation.

Type	Form	Type	Form
Modulus	%=	Shift Right	>>=
Addition	+=	Shift Left	<<=
Subtraction	-=	Bitwise AND	&=
Multiplication	*=	Exclusive OR	^=
Division	/=	Bitwise OR	|=

Figure 2.13 Summary of assignment operators exclusive of simple assignment

You will note that the first expression not only is easier to read, but often executes much faster because the expression is evaluated only once.

For more information on each of the assignment operators, see the section titled *Corresponding Binary Operator*.

Comma Operator ,

The comma operator provides a convenient way to force the evaluation of expressions. If two expressions **expr1** and **expr2** are comma operator operands as in:

```
expr1, expr2
```

then **expr1** is fully evaluated, and subsequently **expr2** is fully evaluated. The type and value of the entire expression is the type and value of **expr2**.

The comma operator is primarily used in **for** statements. It should not be confused with the comma separator used to separate actual parameters in function calls. Because actual parameters are separated by comma separators, the actual parameter expressions may be evaluated in any order.

Also, see the section titled *Statements*.

Preprocessor and Statement Reference

- **Preprocessor Directives**
- **Expressions**
- **lvalues and rvalues**
- **Evaluation Order of Expressions**
- **Statements**

C Preprocessor Directives

Technically, the C preprocessor is not part of the C language. All preprocessor directives are preceded by a #, which should be the first non-whitespace character on the line. For maximum portability, the # should appear in column 1 with no intervening space(s) between it and the preprocessor directive. As a direct consequence, even though conditional preprocessor expressions can be nested, they should not be indented for portability considerations.

Finally, prior to X3J11, the /**/ symbol could be used to concatenate two arguments. As an example:

```
#define smash(a,b) a/**/b          /* a and b become a single token */
```

previously combined two tokens into one. This practice is now invalid and is replaced with the approach of

```
#define smash(a,b) a#b             /* a and b become a single token */
```

define

Use:

Creates preprocessor macros and preprocessor identifiers with optional, associated, text-replacement strings.

Examples:

```
#define DEBUG
#define MSG     "This is a message"
#define macro(a, b, c) ( (a) / ((b) + (c)) )
```

Comments:

The **#define** preprocessor directive is used in three contexts.

1.   Defining the existence of a preprocessor identifier.

2. Defining the existence of a preprocessor identifier and associating a character string that the preprocessor substitutes for each subsequent occurrence of the identifier.

3. Defining a macro that the preprocessor expands into C source code.

While the first two uses are subsets of the third, they will be discussed separately for clarity. In all instances, the identifiers are case-sensitive, just as C identifiers are. However, prevailing convention dictates they be completely capitalized to distinguish them from other program identifiers. Such identifiers are generally referred to as "manifest constants". Finally, some preprocessors consider it an error to define a preprocessor identifier that is already defined, while others allow the previous definition(s) to be stacked and reinstated by subsequent corresponding **#undef** directives.

Defining preprocessor identifiers

Preprocessor identifiers are created by a **#define** directive followed by one or more whitespace characters followed by a unique identifier. The identifier should not be followed by a semi-colon. As an example:

```
/* no semicolon or text follows identifier; avoid comments on same line */
#define DEBUG
```

defines the existence of a preprocessor identifier **DEBUG**. You may use identifiers created in this manner in subsequent **#ifdef**, **#ifndef**, **defined** tests and **#undef** preprocessor directives. In such instances, these identifiers are replaced with a value that evaluates as true (non-zero). Such identifiers are also useful for creating synonyms for basic data types but lack the generality of the **typedef** keyword. Finally, one may use this type identifier as indicated in the following example.

```
#define THEN              /* no value provided */

   if (i==2) THEN exit(); /* THEN is replaced by a NULL string & ignored */
```

One can usually create this type preprocessor identifier by invoking the complier with a **-D** flag. As an example; this would be equivalent to:

```
cc prog1.c -DDEBUG
```

Note that some compilers force all identifiers created in this manner to upper case. In this case:

```
cc prog1.c -DDEBUG
```

would be equivalent to:

```
cc prog1.c -Ddebug
```

Defining Preprocessor Identifiers and Associated Replacement Strings

This application of preprocessor identifier definition can help isolate machine-dependent considerations to a small area of a program such as an include file. This increases code portability. Define preprocessor identifiers just as in the previous example and associate text with an identifier as indicated in the examples in Figure 3.1.

```
#define BITS_IN_A_CHAR   8                               /* machine dependent */
#define BITS_IN_AN_INT   ((sizeof(int))*BITS_IN_A_CHAR)    /* independent */
#define BITS_IN_A_SHORT  ((sizeof(short))*BITS_IN_A_CHAR)  /* independent */
#define BITS_IN_A_LONG   ((sizeof(long))*BITS_IN_A_CHAR)   /* independent */

#define AND              &&              /* use in conditional tests */
#define OR               ||·             /* use in conditional tests */
#define EQUALS           ==              /* use in conditional tests */

#define CHAR1            A               /* valid but suspicious      */
#define CHAR2            "CHAR1"         /* error? - not modified!*    */
#define CHAR3            'A'             /* valid                     */

#define STRING1           hello there....   /* valid but suspicious      */
#define STRING2          "STRING1"          /* error? - not modified!*   */
#define STRING3          "hello there...."  /* valid                     */
#define MAX_STRING_SIZE  (sizeof(STRING3))  /* uses a previous def.      */

#define MAX_WIDTH   20                     /* no = or semicolon   */
#define MAX_HEIGHT  20                     /* no = or semicolon   */
#define MAX_AREA    ((MAX_WIDTH)*(MAX_HEIGHT))  /* note parentheses    */
*Substitutions do not occur within single or double quoted constants/strings.
```

Figure 3.1 Using the preprocessor to increase code portability

As indicated, the identifier definitions should not contain unintended equal signs or semicolons; they will be treated as part of the replacement string. That is:

```
#define MAX_WIDTH = 20;     /* NO NO; NO EQUAL SIGN, NO SEMICOLON */
```

is incorrect on both counts because, wherever possible, the preprocessor substitutes the characters "= 20;" for MAX__WIDTH instead of the characters "20". (Note that substitutions do not occur within single- or double-quoted constants/strings). Subsequent definitions can contain earlier defined identifiers. To avoid precedence problems, any text replacement string that contains an operator should be enclosed in parentheses as should any preprocessor identifier it contains.

If an identifier's replacement string does not fit on one line, it can be extended on the following line by terminating the current line with a line continuation (\ ) character. The definition continues on the first column of the following line.

One can usually create this type preprocessor identifier by invoking the complier with a **-D** flag. As an example:

```
cc prog1.c -DMAX_WIDTH=20
```

is equivalent to the program statement:

```
#define MAX_WIDTH 20
```

A useful way to cater to the possibility of changing parameter values through the **-D** option is as follows:

```
#ifndef MAX_WIDTH
#define MAX_WIDTH   20
#endif
```

Then, defining MAX__WIDTH through the **-D** option will cleanly override the internal default value (20) specified in the program.

Note that some compilers force all identifiers created from compiler flags to upper case as described above.

Finally, note that the preprocessor's replacement of an identifier with an associated string is done from the point of definition within a file until the identifier is undefined or redefined.

As an example, the code in Figure 3.2:

prints:

```
VALUE = 0, j = 0
VALUE = 1, j = 1
VALUE = 0, j = 1
VALUE = 1, j = 1
```

not:

```
VALUE = 0, j = 0
VALUE = 1, j = 1
VALUE = 1, j = 1
VALUE = 1, j = 1
```

despite the fact that the lower loop logic extends beyond a redefinition of VALUE while the original definition precedes the entire loop.

```
int i, j;

#define VALUE 0                              /* first values  */
    j = 0;

    for( i = 0; i < 2; i++ )  {

    printf("\nVALUE = %d, j = %d", VALUE, j);

#undef  VALUE                                /* may be unnecessary */
#define VALUE 1                              /* second values      */
    j = 1;

    printf("\nVALUE = %d, j = %d", VALUE, j);
    }
```

Figure 3.2 Positional effect of the # define preprocessor identifier definition

Defining Preprocessor Macros

Preprocessor directives that define preprocessor macros are distinguished from the above definitions by an opening parenthesis that follows the preprocessor identifier *without intervening whitespace*. Whenever a preprocessor identifier is followed by a whitespace character, it is *not* considered a macro requiring expansion, but only an identifier with an associated replacement string. Again, the definitions should not contain unintended equal signs or semicolons. As an example, consider both:

```
#define square1(x)   ((x) * (x))
#define square2 (x)   ((x) * (x))
```

The first is a macro definition, the second is merely an identifier definition with a replacement string. Note however, that:

```
y = square1(z);        /* no space before parentheses */
y = square1 (z);       /* space before parentheses    */
```

are equivalent. Thus, the space consideration only applies to the macro definition, not subsequent invocations.

If an identifier's replacement string does not fit on one line, it can be extended on the following line by terminating the current line with a backslash (\ ) character. The definition continues on the first column of the following line.

An example of a preprocessor macro definition is:

```
#define abs(x) (((x) < 0) ? -(x) : (x))    /* abs (x) would be wrong */
        └────────────── no whitespace !!!
```

The macro would be invoked with a statement such as:

```
x = abs(3*y+4*z);        /* x gets the absolute value */
```

This macro invocation would fail in execution if the macro definition were not so heavily parenthesized, or in compilation, if there were whitespace between the macro's identifier and the opening parenthesis preceding the **x**.

As a second example, consider the macro definition:

```
#define max_abs(a, b) (((abs(b)) - (abs(a))) < 0) ? (abs(a)) : (abs(b))
```

This macro definition contains more than one input parameter. Note that whitespace is allowed within the parentheses of the macro argument list.

Macros vs. Functions

Macros can closely resemble function calls. Because they avoid the overhead of a function call, they may be faster. However, the speed advantage may be negated by duplicate evaluation of the macro parameter **a** or **b** as indicated in the last example. Moreover, macros result in in-line code expansion at every occurrence, which can exceed the code size required for a function call. In contrast to functions, one cannot take the address of a macro. Finally, macros can be tricky to write and debug because of parentheses considerations and potential, multiple side effects. As an example, all of the following macros have hazards:

```
#define comp1(a, b, c)  a+b*c       /* DANGER: 4 * comp1(1, 2, 3)  fails */
#define comp2(a, b, c) (a+b*c)      /* DANGER: comp2( 1, 2+3, 4+5) fails */
#define comp3(a, b)    ((a)+(b)*(a))  /* comp3(i++, 2)        fails */
```

However, one major advantage of macros is that they do not require the casting of arguments that corresponding functions might require.

Reference:

#ifndef, defined, #ifdef, and **#undef**

defined

Use:

The **defined** operator can appear only in **#if** and **#elif** preprocessor statements. It tests for the existence of a pre-processor identifier definition and produces a value of 1 (TRUE) or zero (FALSE). The **defined** operator has the same precedence as primary expression operators.

Examples:

`#define TEST_ID`
 	
`#if defined(TEST_ID)`
`#define TESTING`
`#endif`
	`#undef  TESTX`
	`#define TEST_ID`
	
	`#ifdef  TESTX`
	`#define TESTINGX`
	`#elif defined(TEST_ID)`
	`#define TESTINGX`
	`#endif`

`#if !defined(TESTX) || defined(TEST_ID)`
`#define DEBUG`
`#endif`	

Comments:

This preprocessor operator is extremely powerful and allows complex expressions to be built that would otherwise require preprocessor directive nesting. It is also new and does not appear in many compilers, but is required with X3J11.

Reference:

#define, #undef

#elif/#else

Use:

The **elif** directive is used in place of an **#else** directive to simplify nested **#if, #ifdef,** and **#ifndef** preprocessor operations. The **elif** directive allows conditional inclusion of source statements within a compilation. It corresponds to the C language **else if** construct, is relatively new, and does not appear in many compilers.

Format:

```
#if    const-expr1
   < lines included if const-expr1 is non-zero >
#elif const-expr2
   < lines included if const-expr2 is non-zero >
#elif const-expr3
   < lines included if const-expr3 is non-zero >
#else
   < lines included if const-expr3 is zero >
#endif
```

Note that only one **#endif** directive was required even though three conditional directives were nested.

Example:

```
#if    DEBUG_LEVEL == 1
#include "test1.c"

#elif DEBUG_LEVEL == 2  ]|  defined(TEST2)
#include "level2.c"

#elif DEBUG_LEVEL == 3  && !defined(TESTING)
#include "level3.c"

#else
#include "stdinc.c"

#endif
```

Comments:

The **#elif** directive allows conditional inclusion of source-code statements within a program compilation and corresponds to the C language **else if** combination. Selection of statements following an **#elif** directive occurs when the corresponding constant expression associated with the **#elif** is true (non-zero).

All statements following the **#elif** are included up to the next **#elif, #else,** or **#endif** directive. Once a condition evaluates to a true (non-zero) value and all associated source statements are included, the preprocessor discards all statements between the last statement included and the end of the entire construct. Thus, at most one group of source statements is selected in any **#if, #elif,** and **#else** program construct.

Note that the use of the **#elif** directive is discretionary because its effect may be achieved using multiple **#if, #else,** and **#endif** combinations. That is, the constructs in Figure 3.3 are equivalent.

Finally, note that even though conditional expressions can be nested, they should not be indented for portability considerations.

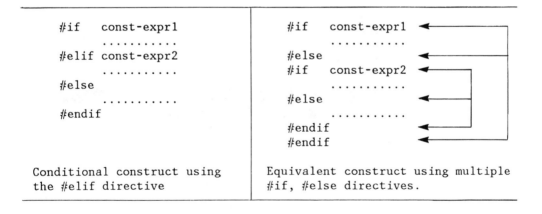

```
#if    const-expr1            #if    const-expr1
      ..........                    ..........
#elif const-expr2             #else
      ..........              #if    const-expr2
#else                               ..........
      ..........              #else
#endif                              ..........
                             #endif
                             #endif

Conditional construct using    Equivalent construct using multiple
the #elif directive            #if, #else directives.
```

Figure 3.3 Comparing the # if / # else and # if / # elif preprocessor constructs

Reference:

#else, #endif, and **#if**

#else

Use:

The **#else** directive is used to provide alternative inclusion capability in **#if, #ifdef,** and **#ifndef** preprocessor constructs.

Reference:

#eif, #ifdef, and **#ifndef**

#endif

Use:

The **#endif** directive is used to terminate **#if, #ifdef,** and **#ifndef** preprocessor constructs.

Reference:

#if, #ifdef, and **#ifndef**

#if

Use:

The **#if** directive allows source statements to be conditionally included in a program. The directive evaluates an expression and tests whether a condition is TRUE (non-zero). Thus, in UNIX:

```
cc -DDEBUG   prog1.c
```

is always equivalent to:

```
cc -DDEBUG=1 prog1.c
```

Format:

```
#if    const-expr
    < lines included if const-expr is true (non-zero) >
#else      /* a #else is optional */
    < lines included if const-expr is false (zero)    >
#endif
```

Examples:

```
#if DEBUG_LEVEL == 3   && !defined(TESTING)
#include "level3.c"
#else
#include "stdinc.c"
#endif

#if DEBUG
    printf("\nIEH4033I - SYS1.ERROR\n");
#endif
```

Comments:

The **#if** directive allows source statements to be conditionally included in a program. Selection of statements following a **#if** directive occurs when the corresponding constant expression associated with the **#if** is true (non-zero).

All statements following the **#if** are included up to the next **#elif, #else**, or **#endif** directive. Once a condition evaluates to a true (non-zero) value and all associated source statements are included, the preprocessor discards all statements between the last statement included and the end of the entire construct. Thus, at most one group of source statements is selected in any **#if, #elif,** and **#else** program construct. The preprocessor does not observe statement grouping by braces. Therefore, the groups are delineated by the **#elif, #else,** or **#endif** directives.

Conditional expressions can be nested as indicated in Figure 3.4.

Even though conditional expressions can be nested, they should not be indented for portability considerations.

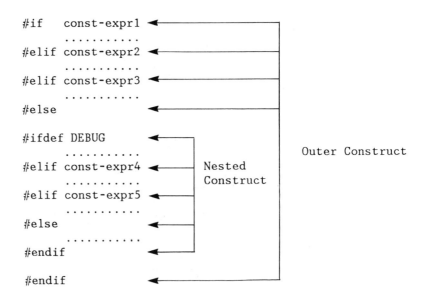

Figure 3.4 Nesting conditional preprocessor constructs

Reference:

#elif and **#else**

#ifdef

Use:

The **#ifdef** preprocessor directive tests for the definition of a preprocessor identifier, allowing conditional inclusion of source statements if the preprocessor identifier is defined. Unlike the **#if** directive, the **#ifdef** directive does not test the value of an argument, it only tests if an argument is defined.

Format:

```
#ifdef identifier
       < statements to include if the identifier exists >
#else           /* a #else is optional */
       < statements to include if the identifier does not exist >
#endif
```

Example:

Figure 3.5 shows how to use the preprocessor **#ifdef** directive to include the conditional test drive code.

```
test_print(str)  /* a small function */
char *str;
{
  printf("%s",str);
}

#ifdef DEBUG      /* include a test driver to test a function */
main()
{
  test_print("hello\n");
}
#endif
```

Figure 3.5 Using the preprocessor # ifdef directive to include conditional test driver code

Comments:

The **#ifdef** preprocessor directive is a variant of the **#if** preprocessor directive. A given instance of a **#if** preprocessor directive can be nested with other **#if, #ifdef,** and **#ifndef** preprocessor directives. If the identifier is defined, all statements following the **#ifdef** are included up to the next corresponding **#else, #elif,** or **#endif.**

The effect of the **#ifdef** preprocessor directive can be achieved by a combination of the **#if** preprocessor directive and the **defined** operator, as follows:

```
#ifdef TEST              /* one way to do it      */
      < statements to include if the identifier exists >
#endif

#if defined(TEST)        /* another way to do it */
      < statements to include if the identifier exists >
#endif
```

Reference:
#define, #if, #ifndef, and **#undef**

#ifndef

Use:

The **#ifndef** preprocessor directive tests for the definition of a preprocessor identifier and allows conditional inclusion of source statements if the preprocessor identifier is *not* defined. Unlike the **#if** directive, the **#ifndef** directive does not test the value of an argument, it only tests if an argument is NOT defined.

Format:

```
#ifndef identifier
      < statements to include if the identifier does not exist >
#else         /* a #else is optional */
      < statements to include if the identifier exists >
#endif
```

Example:

Figure 3.6 shows how to use the preprocessor **#ifndef** directive to include conditional test drive code.

```
test_print(str)      /* a small function */
char *str;
{
  printf("%s",str);
}

#ifndef PRODUCTION /* include a test driver to test a function */
main()
{
  test_print("hello\n");
}
#endif
```

Figure 3.6 Using the preprocessor # ifndef directive to include conditional test driver code

Comments:

The **#ifndef** preprocessor directive is a variant of the **#if** preprocessor directive. A given instance of a **#endif** preprocessor directive can be nested with other **#if, #ifdef,** and **#ifndef** preprocessor directives. If the identifier is *not* defined, all statements following the **#ifndef** are included up to the next corresponding **#else, #elif,** or **#endif.**

The effect of the **#ifndef** preprocessor directive can be achieved by a combination of the **#if** preprocessor directive and the **defined** and **!** operators, as follows:

```
#ifndef TEST            /* one way to do it      */
     < statements to include if the identifier does not exist >
#endif

#if !defined(TEST)      /* another way to do it */
     < statements to include if the identifier does not exist >
#endif
```

Reference:

#define, #if, #ifdef, and **#undef**

#include

Use:

The **#include** preprocessor directive allows inclusion of source files within a source file.

Format:

```
#include "file"    /* "..." ==> search user, then system libraries */
#include <file>    /* <...> ==> search system libraries only       */
```

Examples:

```
#include "functn1.c"   /* "..." ==> search user, then system libraries */
#include <functn2.c>   /* <...> ==> search system libraries only       */
```

Comments:

#include preprocessor directives can be nested, but use caution for code control considerations. Moreover, definition and/or initialization of objects should be carefully considered if a file is included in more than one program file. Finally, statements in one included file should not refer to values defined in a subsequent included file due to limitations of the preprocessor.

To avoid including a file more than once in a program that includes nested files, consider the technique shown in Figure 3.7.

The effect of the **#include** preprocessor directive can be achieved with a **-i** flag on some compilers.

```
                    /* This is include file 1012          */
                    /* first test to see if already included */
#ifndef  UNIQUE_FILE_1012
                    /* if not defined, then include        */
                        .   .   .

          <include data>
                              .   .   .
#define UNIQUE_FILE_1012
#endif
```

Figure 3.7 Avoiding re-inclusion of an include file

#line

Use:

The **#line** preprocessor directive forces the compiler to reset its line input counter to a new value and optionally associate the input with a new file name.

Format:

#line constant optional-file-name

Example:

```
#line 45 funct4.c
```

Comments:

This preprocessor directive is mainly used by C language program-file generators and/or preprocessors. It assists in the debugging process because compiler-source input errors are usually identified by file name and line number. If the optional file name is missing, the line input number is modified and the file name remains the same.

#undef

Use:

The **#undef** directive removes the current definition of a pre-processor identifier. It may be used with arguments that are not previously **#define**d.

Format:

#undef identifier

Examples:

```
#undef DEBUG
#undef TEST
```

Comments:

No text follows the identifier being undefined. An identifier can be undefined with impunity, even if it has not yet been defined. Some compilers stack preprocessor definitions associated with a preprocessor identifier. In such cases, a **#undef** directive will unstack the last, stacked value and consider it the new value of the preprocessor identifier.

This directive is useful if a compiler does not allow an identifier to be defined and if a definition is already in effect. When in doubt, use the following approach:

```
#undef TEST
#define TEST
```

Reference:

#define, #ifdef, and **#ifndef**

Expressions

Expressions are combinations of tokens that produce a value and usually cause *side effects* in the evaluation process. A side effect can be defined as a change in an object's value due to evaluating an expression. For example, in the statement:

$$a = b = 5;$$

The expression:

$$b = 5$$

evaluates to five and has a side effect of setting **b** to five. The fact that the expression evaluates to five allows **a** to be set to five as a side effect of evaluating:

$$a = 5;$$

Note that the expression:

$$(5)$$

causes no side effects.

Side effects happen as a result of:

function calls

assignment expressions

auto-increment expressions

auto-decrement expressions

Some side effects are extremely subtle. Suppose that **int__ptr** is a pointer to a memory-mapped I/O device and that every reference to ***int__ptr** causes an interrupt to be generated on a slave machine. The expressions:

```
(*int_ptr)++;   -and-   *int_ptr += 1;    /* one memory reference */
```

can have dramatically different side effects than does:

```
*int_ptr = *int_ptr+1;   /* two memory references possible */
```

Moreover, such expressions must not be optimized out of loops as illustrated in Figure 3.8. Use of the X3J11 keyword **volatile** prevents this form of incorrect code optimization.

Expressions have the type(s) of their token(s). One could use an object of type **t** whenever one can use an expression of type **t** except in certain contexts, such as array bounds, where constant expressions are required.

```
for (i=0; i<10; i++)
        *int_ptr;              /* do not optimize out */
```

Figure 3.8 Non optimized loop preserving side effects of a volatile object

lvalues and rvalues

An **lvalue** is an expression that refers to the location of an object. Specifically, an **lvalue** is:

1. an identifier, or

2. the result of the indirection operator, or

3. the result of the member selection operator **.** when the left-hand operand is an **lvalue.**

The value of an object is alterable (via assignment, auto-increment, and auto-decrement) only by using an **lvalue** to access it.

Since **a[b]** is equivalent to **(*(a + b))**, subscript expressions are **lvalues**. Moreover, since **a->b** is equivalent to **(*a).b**, the result of the **->** is also an **lvalue** .

An **rvalue** is an expression that permits retrieval and/or examination of a value, but does not allow alteration of the value.

```
int *ptr, x[3] = { 0, 1, 2 }, a;
         x[0] = x[1] + x[2];
         x[0] = 2 + 3;
```

```
              lvalues              rvalues
              -----------          -----------
              ptr, *ptr                x
                 *x                   2 + 3
                x[0]              x[1] + x[2]
```

Figure 3.9 Examples of lvalues and rvalues

Evaluation Order of Expressions

C does not specify the evaluation order of operands. As an example, consider the functions in Figure 3.10.

```
#include "stdio.h"

main()
{
    printf ("\nTotal = %d", fun(1)+fun(2) );
}

fun(i)
int i;
{
  printf("\nReturning %d",i);
  return(i);
}
```

Figure 3.10 Ambiguity of operand evaluation

The example code could generate either set of output illustrated in Figure 3.11 depending on the compiler.

```
Returning 1                      Returning 2
Returning 2        -or-          Returning 1
Total = 3                        Total = 3
```

Figure 3.11 Possible output from Figure 3.10 code

Thus it is not advisable to write code that depends on the order of side effects within a statement. Any point in which all side effects are guaranteed to be complete is called a *synch point*. Synch points only occur at statement completion and with the comma, conditional, and logical connective (&&) operators. A final, hazardous example of side-effect sequencing is found in the statement:

```
a[i] = i++;
```

Beware that the auto-increment and auto-decrement operators result in assignments. In general, never use an **lvalue** more than once in an expression if an instance of its use results in an assignment to the **lvalue** . Finally, remember that function calls are expressions and, therefore, their formal arguments are subject to the same consideration.

Statements

Individual statements are terminated with semicolons. They may be continued on another line at any point whitespace is allowed (except for character-string definitions that must be terminated by a line-continuation character with the definition resuming in column 1 of the next line.) There are many forms of statements. They are:

null (a stand-alone semicolon)

expression (a valid expression followed by a semicolon)

block/compound

break

continue

do

for

goto

if

return

switch

while

In block/compound statements, one or more valid statements are enclosed in braces. The closing brace is not followed by a semicolon. Automatic and static variables may be optionally defined and initialized after the opening brace. The scope of such variables is local to the block. Block/compound statements can be nested and are allowed anywhere a simple statement is allowed.

break

Use:

A **break** statement immediately terminates an innermost **do, for, switch,** or **while** statement.

Format:

break;

Examples:

Figure 3.12 shows how to use the break statement in loop constructs.

Comments:

Execution resumes at the first statement following the terminated **do, for, switch,** or **while** statement. In contrast, when a **continue** statement is used in a **do, for,** or **while** statement, only the current iteration of the loop is terminated.

A **break** statement is equivalent to a **goto** statement that branches to an appropriately labeled null statement immediately following the terminated statement.

```
     j = 0;
do {
    i = fgetc(file_ptr);
    if ( i == EOF )
       break; ─────────┐
       . . . . .       │
       j++;            │
} while (j < 1000);    │
◄──────────────────────┘
       . . . . .
```

```
for( j = 0; j < 1000; j++) {
    i = fgetc(file_ptr);
    if ( i == EOF )
       break; ─────────────┐
       . . . . .           │
    r = s + x;             │
}                          │
◄──────────────────────────┘
       . . . . .
```

```
     j = 0;
while (j < 1000) {
    j++;
    i = fgetc(file_ptr);
    if ( i == EOF )
       break; ─────────┐
       . . . . .       │
    r = s + x;         │
}                      │
◄──────────────────────┘
       . . . . .
```

```
switch ( i = fgetc(file_ptr) ) {

    case EOF : break; ───────────────┐
                                     │
    case  27 : beep();               │
               break; ───────────────┤
       . . . . .                     │
    default  : r = s + x;            │
}                                    │
◄────────────────────────────────────┘
       . . . . .
```

Figure 3.12 Using the break statement in loop constructs

Reference:

continue, do, for, return, while and **switch**

continue

Use:

The **continue** immediately terminates the current iteration of an innermost **do, for,** or **while** block statement.

Format:

continue;

Examples:

Figure 3.13 shows how to use the **continue** statement in loop constructs.

```
     j = 0;
do {
     i = fgetc(file_ptr);
     if ( i == 27 )
        continue; ────────┐
      . . . . .           │
        j++;              │
◄─────────────────────────┘
} while (j < 1000);
      . . . . .
```

```
for( j = 0; j < 1000; j++) {
     i = fgetc(file_ptr);
     if ( i == 27 )
        continue; ────────┐
      . . . . .           │
     r = s + x;          │
◄─────────────────────────┘
}
      . . . . .
```

```
     j = 0;
while (j < 1000) {
     j++;
     i = fgetc(file_ptr);
     if ( i == EOF )
        continue; ────────┐
      . . . . .           │
     r = s + x;          │
◄─────────────────────────┘
}
      . . . . .
```

Figure 3.13 Using the continue statement in loop constructs

Comments:

In the case of a **do** or **while** statement, execution resumes at the loop continuation test. In the case of a **for** statement, execution resumes at the loop reinitialization step.

In contrast, when a **break** statement is used in a **do, for,** or **while** statement, the entire **do, for,** or **while** statement is terminated.

If a **switch**'s **case** statement contains a **continue** associated with a **do**, **for**, or **while** statement that is not enclosed within the **case** statement, then the switch statement should be enclosed within an associated **do, while** or **for** statement.

A **continue** statement is equivalent to a **goto** statement that branches to an appropriately labeled null statement immediately preceding the closing brace of the **do, for,** or **while** statement.

Reference:

break, do, for, return, while

do

Use:

the **do** statement provides a loop construct with a trailing test.

Format:

```
    Block                                    Simple

do {                                      do
    statement /* body of loop */              statement        /* body of loop */
    statement /* body of loop */          while (condition);
    . . . . .
} while (condition);

                    required semicolon
```

Examples:

Figure 3.14 shows examples of the **do** statement.

```
    j = 0;
do {
    i = fgetc(file_ptr);
    if ( i == 27 )
        continue;
    . . . . .
        j++;
} while (j < 1000);
    . . . . .
```

```
    j = 0;
do }
    i = fgetc(file_ptr);
    if ( i == EOF )
        break;
    . . . . .
        j++;
} while (j < 1000);
    . . . . .
```

```
do
    i = getchar();
while ( i < 61);
```

Figure 3.14 Examples of the do statement

Comments:

The statement (simple or compound) is executed. A loop body must be present, though it may be a null statement. The trailing test is performed to determine if another iteration of the loop should occur. If the test results in a true condition (evaluates to a non-zero value), another iteration is performed. Iterations continue until the trailing test is found to be false (equal to zero).

The statement is always executed once. Figure 3.15 shows the logic in a flow chart.

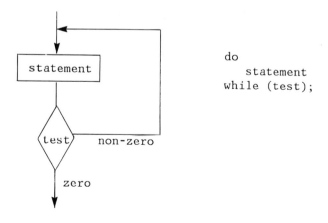

```
do
    statement
while (test);
```

Figure 3.15 do statement flow chart

Hazards:

Beware of using $=$ instead of $==$ and using bitwise operators instead of logical connective operators within the condition test.

Reference:

break, continue, for, return, while

for

Use:

The **for** statement provides a leading-test looping construct with initialization and reinitialization provisions.

Format:

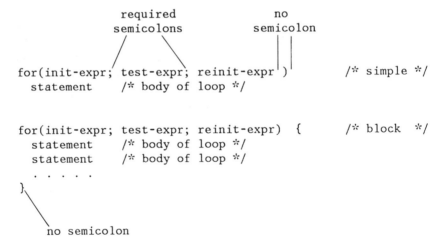

```
                      required                  no
                      semicolons           semicolon
                         /        \           |  |
for(init-expr; test-expr; reinit-expr )          /* simple */
    statement     /* body of loop */

for(init-expr; test-expr; reinit-expr) {        /* block */
    statement     /* body of loop */
    statement     /* body of loop */
    . . . . .
}
      \
       no semicolon
```

Note: init-expr, test-expr, and reinit-expr are all optional.

Examples:

```
for ( ; ; )  /* no expressions */
 if ( (i = getchar() ) == 27 )
    break;
```

```
for (init-expr; ;reinit-expr)  -equivalent to-  for (init-expr;1 ;reinit-expr)
 if ( (i = getchar() ) == 27 )                     if ( (i = getchar() ) == 27 )
    break;                                            break;
```

```
for( j = 0; j < 1000; j++) {          for( j = 0; j < 1000; j++) }
    i = fgetc(file_ptr);                  i = fgetc(file_ptr);
    if ( i == 27 )                        if ( i == EOF )
       continue; ──────────              break; ──────────
       . . . . .                            . . . . .
    r = s + x;                            r = s + x;
   ◄─                                     }
 }                                    ◄─
   . . . . .                             . . . . .
```

Figure 3.16 Examples of the for statement

Comments:

The initial expression is evaluated. The test expression is then evaluated. If it is true (evaluates to non-zero), the loop body is executed. If it is false (evaluates to zero), the loop is terminated. A loop body must be present, though it may be a null statement.

After each execution of the loop statement, the reinitialization expression is evaluated. The test expression is evaluated again and the loop statement is executed again depending on the result of the evaluation. The loop statement continues to be executed until the test expression evaluates to zero, or a **break**, **goto** or **return** statement is executed.

The initialization, test, and reinitialization expressions may each consist of multiple expressions separated by the comma operator and are all optional. However, the separator semi-colons still must be present if either the initialization or test expression(s) is absent.

The value of the loop control variable(s) can be changed within the loop statement and is retained after termination of the **for** statement.

Because the test is a leading test, the loop might never be executed. Figure 3.17 shows the logic in a flow chart.

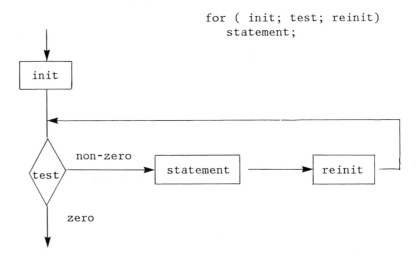

```
for ( init; test; reinit)
      statement;
```

Figure 3.17 for statement flow chart

A beautiful use of the **for** statement is in linked-list processing. As an example, see Figure 3.18.

```
struct Node { .....
             .....
         struct Node *NextNode;   /* pointer to next node in list */
         };

struct Node *ListHead;                  /* anchor point for linked list */

for (p = ListHead; p; p = p -> NextNode)
         . . . .          /* process node */
```

Figure 3.18 Classic use of the for statement with imbedded recursive structure pointers

Hazards:

Beware of using = instead of = =; using bitwise operators instead of logical connective operators within the condition test; inadvertent use of semicolon after the closing parenthesis of the **for**; and missing braces on block loop statements.

Reference:

break, continue, do, return, while

goto

Use:

The **goto** statement forces an immediate branch to a labeled statement within the currently executing function.

Format:

```
          . . . . .
          goto label;
          . . . . .

    label:   statement
                \
                 \
                  required colon on label
```

Examples:

```
        . . . . .
        goto label1;
        . . . . .
label1:  ;   /* label must precede a stmt, null stmt used here */
```

Comments:

Since labels have local scope, a **goto** can only branch within the same function. The **goto** is useful in exiting deeply nested program constructs. However, its use should be avoided.

Hazards:

The **goto** statement makes programs difficult to read, understand, modify, and maintain. Because program labels do not have block scope as do local variables, a **goto** may bypass program logic that initializes local block variables, as shown in Figure 3.19.

```
funcx()
{ int a=3;
  goto lab2;
      { int a=10;                /* new block              */
 lab2: printf(" a=%d",a);        /* prints "a=3"          · */
        return;                  /* exits entire function */
      }
}
```

Figure 3.19 goto statement initialization-bypass hazard

if

Use:

The **if** statement allows conditional execution of program statements.

Format:

Figure 3.20 shows the format of the **if** statement.

```
              no semicolon                                 no semicolon
                  /|                                           /|
if (test-expr)                           if (test-expr)    {
   statement1                               statement1
else              /* optional */            statement2     /* optional */
   statement2                               . . . . .      /* optional */
                                         }
                                         else {            /* optional */
                                            statement3
                                            statement4     /* optional */
                                            . . . . .
                                         }

        Simple                                        Block
```

Figure 3.20 Format of the if statement

Examples:

Figure 3.21 shows an example of an **if** statement.

```
if ( i == EOF )                  c = getchar();
    return(0);                   if ( isupper(c) ) {
else {                               beep();
   process(i);                       log_error();
   goodmsg(i);                   }
}                                else {
                                     process(c);
                                     goodmsg(c);
                                 }
```

Figure 3.21 Example of an if statement

Comments:

The test expression is evaluated. If it is true (evaluates to a non-zero value), the statement associated with the **if** is executed. If the expression is false (evaluates to zero), the statement associated with the optional **else**, if any, is executed.

The optional **else** is paired with the last **if** that does not have an associated **else**, unless otherwise indicated by braces.

Figure 3.22 shows the logic in a flow chart.

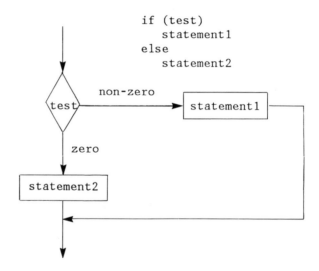

```
if (test)
    statement1
else
    statement2
```

Figure 3.22 if statement flow chart

The **else** may consist of another **if** statement. This conditional cascading is referred to as an **else if** construct, as shown in the flow chart in Figure 3.23.

Note that once a test evaluates as true, the statement associated with it is executed and the construct processing is terminated.

```
if (test1)
    statement1
else if (test2)
    statement2
else if (test3)
    statement3
else  /* default */
    statement4
```

Figure 3.23 Nested if statement flow chart

Hazards:

Beware of using $=$ instead of $==$; using bitwise operators instead of logical connective operators within the condition test; inadvertent use of semicolon after the closing parenthesis of the **if** test condition; and missing braces on block statements. When supplied, make sure braces are correctly supplied for nested **if** statements as shown in Figure 3.24.

```
      if (test1)                            if (test1) {
        if (test2) {                           if (test2) {
            statement1                             statement1
            statement2                             statement2
        }                                      }
      else {                                 }
            statement3                       else {
            statement4                           statement3
        }                                        statement4
                                             }

MISLEADING INDENTATION           NON-MISLEADING BRACING AND INDENTATION
```

Figure 3.24 Misleading indentation hazard

return

Use:

The **return** statement immediately terminates an executing function even from within an executing loop(s).

Format:

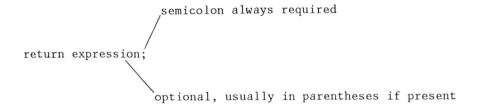

```
                         semicolon always required


      return expression;

                         optional, usually in parentheses if present
```

Examples:

```
return;       /* returned value unpredictable    */
return 0;     /* zero is cast to the function type */
return (0);   /* zero is cast to the function type */
return (-1);  /* -1 is cast to the function type   */
```

Comments:

The function is immediately terminated even if one or more **do,** **for,** or **while** loops are in progress. If possible, the optional value, if any, associated with the **return** is cast to the type of the function and returned back to the calling function. Otherwise, the returned value is undefined, or, in the case where the optional value cannot be correctly cast, a compiler error is generated. As an example, if a function returns a structure but the **return** is specified as:

```
return 4;
```

a compiler should generate a complaint.

A **return** without an associated value is automatically issued for functions that "fall off the end of their definition."

Hazards:

Do not **return** a pointer to an automatic object or a function formal parameter.

Reference

break, continue, do, for, while. Also, see *Understanding Mis-declarations Associated with Functions*.

switch

Use:

The **switch** statement provides a multiway branching construct based on constant values.

Format:

Figure 3.25 shows the format for a **switch** statement.

```
                                   required opening brace
                                  /
switch (integer-expr) {
    case constant-1 :       /* single case label associated with code  */
            statement
            break;          /* terminates switch processing            */
    case constant-2 :       /* first case label associated with code   */
    case constant-3 :       /* another case label associated with code */
            statement       /* multiple statements allowed....         */
            statement       /*   ..... without the need for braces     */
            break;          /* terminates switch processing            */
    case constant-4 :
            statement       /* no break ==> falls through here         */
    case constant-5 :
            statement
            break;          /* avoids falling into default code        */
    default :               /* default is optional, has no constant    */
            statement
            break;          /* this break is for defensive programming */
}
  no semicolon
  required closing brace
```

Figure 3.25 switch statement format

Example:

Figure 3.26 shows an example of a **switch** statement.

```
#define VALUE 10

    switch ( i = getchar() ) {
        case 'A' + VALUE : break      /* 'K' */
        case 0x61        : break;     /* 'a' */
        case 'b'         : break;     /* 'b' */
        case 0141        : break;     /* 'c' */
        default          : putchar(i);
    }
          no semicolon
```

Figure 3.26 switch statement example

Comments:

The constants associated with **case** statements are used to build a branch table. Thus a **case** constant can only be used once. The integer (includes **int, long, short** with X3J1l) expression is evaluated and compared against the constant expressions associated with each **case** label. In any event, the constants must be unique.

If a match is found, execution begins at the first executable statement following the matching **case** label. Otherwise, the action associated with an optional **default**, if any, is executed. There is no constant associated with the optional **default**, and the **default** statement does not have to be placed after all **case** statements. If no match is found and there is no **default**, the entire **switch** construct is skipped.

Multiple **case** labels can be associated with a single action. If a single action consists of more than one statement, then the statements need not be enclosed within braces. If a **break** statement does not separate one **case** from an immediately following one, execution of the first **case** action continues into the next **case** action.

If a multiway branch construct is required that is based on ranges of values rather than specific values, use the **if** statement.

Hazards:

Beware of omitting or misplacing a **break**. Do not use floating point expressions as the switch expression or as **case** constants.

Reference:

if

while

Use:

The **while** statement provides a loop construct with a leading test.

Format:

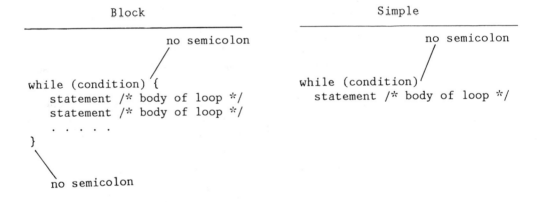

Block

no semicolon

```
while (condition) {
    statement /* body of loop */
    statement /* body of loop */
      . . . . .
}
```

no semicolon

Simple

no semicolon

```
while (condition)
    statement /* body of loop */
```

Examples:

Figure 3.27 shows an example of a **while** statement.

Comments:

The leading test is performed to determine if an iteration of the loop should occur. If the test results in a true condition (evaluates to a non-zero value), an iteration is performed. A loop

```
        j = 0;                          j = 0;
    while (j < 1000) {              while (j < 1000) {
        j++;                            j++;
        i = fgetc(file_ptr);            i = fgetc(file_ptr);
        if ( i == EOF )                 if ( i == EOF )
            continue;                       break;
          . . . . .                       . . . . .
            r = s + x;                      r = s + x;
                                       }
    }

          . . . . .                       . . . . .
```

Figure 3.27 while statement example

statement must be present, though it may be a null statement. The leading test is then performed again to determine if another iteration of the loop should occur. Iterations continue until the leading test is found to be false (equal to zero).

Because the test is a leading test, the loop may never be executed. Figure 3.28 shows the logic in a flow chart.

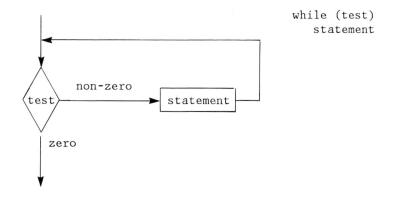

Figure 3.28 while statement flow chart

The **while** and **for** statements are related as shown in Figure 3.29.

```
init;                              for(init; test; reinit)
while (test) {                         statement
  statement
  reinit;
}
```

Figure 3.29 Relationship between the while and for statements (statement cannot contain a continue)

Hazards:

Beware of using = instead of = =; using bitwise operators instead of logical connective operators within the condition test; inadvertent use of semicolon after the closing parenthesis of the **while** test condition; and missing braces on block loop statements.

Reference:

break, continue, do, for, return

(Non) Standard Library File I/O Function Portability

File I/O is not part of the C language. File I/O is achieved via library functions that accompany each compiler. C compilers were written by a variety of dispersed groups for a spectrum of machines with a variety of hardware architectures, peripheral devices, and operating systems. Therefore, portability problems typically exist for C programs involving file I/O.

The portability problems also appear to have arisen partly as a result of having compiler run-time libraries attempt to mimic UNIX's, low-level I/O functions when the libraries native operating system had different file I/O notions than UNIX, primarily in the area of file structure. Traditionally, the implementers achieved varying degrees of success. The areas that could not be addressed introduced a variety of portability situations.

Symptoms of the portability problem appear as identically named functions providing different services, functions having different names providing identical services, and functions that are unique for given systems. Finally, functions can have identical names, and provide identical services, but still require different formal parameters.

In summary, compiler compatibility in the area of file I/O functions is best described as modest but sharing a UNIX flavor. The following discussion must therefore be viewed as conceptual rather than definitive, though most of it will often apply to any given environment. Your compiler's library is your definitive guide to file I/O. It is hoped the ANSI X3J11 C Standards Committee effort will significantly relieve this situation.

Standard I/O Concepts

The prevailing C library perspective of file processing is heavily influenced by UNIX. Consequently, two levels of processing are associated with C library functions, referred to as **low-level file I/O** and **high-level file I/O**. In either level, a file must be opened before it can be processed. The manner in which a file is opened determines the types of services and level of processing (high or low) that can be used on the file. Regardless of the level, you should explicitly close all explicitly opened files when their processing is completed. Finally, be sure to include **stdio.h** in files that use standard I/O functions.

Low-Level (UNIX) File I/O

In low-level file I/O, the associated library functions directly invoke various operating system file services. This level of processing necessarily observes the operating system's view of data files and forfeits a corresponding level of operating system independence in the process. In low-level file I/O, an open file is individually identifiable from other open files by a unique, unsigned integer value, called a **file descriptor**, assigned to the file by the operating system during the open process. A given file may be opened multiple times and at any time. Each instance of the open file would have a unique file descriptor.

Code written for low-level processing often experiences the least degree of portability and higher degrees of complexity, though it can enjoy a greater level of file processing efficiency and flexibility. As an example, both text and binary files can be processed with this level.

High-Level I/O

In high-level file I/O, library functions invoke the more primitive low-level file I/O services. In high-level file I/O, a given file is individually identifiable from other open files by a unique pointer value called a **file pointer**. The file pointer points at a unique file-structure variable associated with the file during the file-opening process.

This approach realizes a corresponding increase in code portability because of the greater isolation from the operating system environment. It achieves this portability at the expense of file-processing flexibility. As an example, binary files cannot be processed with this approach in some environments. Finally, to use high-level file I/O, a program must include **stdio.h** that contains the preprocessor definition of **EOF**, **FILE**, and **NULL** which are necessary for this level of processing.

Low-Level Read Write Position Pointers

In high-level processing, a file is regarded as a continuous sequence of bytes, called a **stream**. Read/write operations typically occur from/to buffers, which are maintained by the high-level file I/O Functions. Thus, the routines keep track of where the next character will be fetched from or placed in the buffer for reads and writes respectively.

In low-level file I/O, the position of the next character(s) within a file to be processed (read or written) is determined by a value, called the file's *read/write position pointer*, sometimes referred to as a file's *character pointer*.

The value of a file's read/write position pointer is updated after each file input/output request and reflects the position where the next file read or write will occur. A file's read/write position pointer is conceptually maintained by the operating system. In some instances, in both high and low-level I/O processing, this value is program resettable, allowing a program to provide processing as opposed to what normally occurs when the read/write position pointer is not explicitly repositioned by the program.

Buffered vs. Unbuffered I/O

Low-level file I/O interfaces directly with the operating system services that maintain a file's read/write position pointer. Each low-level, read/write request is accompanied by information for the particular, desired activity as well as an associated data area that receives/holds the corresponding data. One read/write call conceptually results in one immediate call to the operating system, which could result in an immediate physical read/write to the file if the operating system is not buffering the file.

In contrast, high-level I/O services queue data in buffers in anticipation of future requests. In the case of input files, the various requests are applied against the waiting, buffered data until a new request cannot be completely serviced with the data remaining in the buffer. The high-level I/O routines then refresh the exhausted buffer via a low-level I/O request and service the outstanding request with the previously remaining data plus an appropriate amount of new data. In the case of output data, the data are placed in a buffer until it is filled. The high-level routines then invoke low-level I/O routines to write the buffer out to the file.

Note that some systems allow programs to set the size and location of the buffers used in high-level I/O via a **setbuf** function call. A program may indicate that a buffer size of zero is to be used, in which case no buffering will be done even though the file is processed using high-level processing. If the **setbuf** function is used with an automatic buffer variable, make sure to **fclose** the file and **fflush** the buffer before returning from the owning function. This prevents the system from reusing the buffer area for other processing before the data has been flushed.

As an example, consider:

```
#include "stdio.h"

main()
{
    char buf[BUFSIZE];    /* DANGER ! should be static for safety sake! */
    setbuf(stdout,buf);
        . . . .

}
```

As indicated, buffers should be declared **static** to avoid random, system-defined failures.

Mixing Levels of I/O on a File

When a file is opened for high-level processing, a unique file pointer is associated with the file as are one or more file buffers. The file pointer points to a unique structure variable used by the high-level services. Because the high-level file-processing support invokes low-level file-function calls, one of the members of the file structure variable is often the file's file descriptor required for low-level processing. Thus, it is sometimes possible to deduce the file descriptor for a file opened for high-level processing.

Because of buffering, individual, high-level I/O requests for sequential file processing do not usually result in immediate, physical reads/writes to a file and subsequent updating of the file read/write pointer. Indiscreet low-level function requests using a deduced file descriptor are invisible to high-level services and can cause the operating system to modify a file's read/write position pointer. If the file position pointer has been disturbed by renegade, low-level calls, data that are eventually read from (or written to) a file by a later, high-level I/O request will not sequentially follow data previously read (or written). *Do not mix high-level and low-level service calls on a single open file.* Use of deduced file descriptors in explicit, low-level, file-service calls is guaranteed to corrupt subsequent, high-level calls. The results can be ghastly, though well-deserved. Figure 4.1 shows buffered I/O.

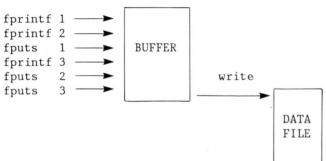

The high-level file I/O requests continue until the corresponding data buffer is full. The data buffer is then written to the file and is reused for the next sequences of high-level file I/O requests.

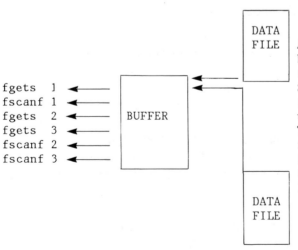

A high-level I/O input buffer is filled when the fopen request completes. Subsequent high-level I/O input requests continue until the buffer is emptied. The buffer is then quietly replenished by a low-level file I/O request issued internally by the high-level I/O routines.

Figure 4.1 Buffered I/O

stdin, stdout, stderr

The files **stdin**, **stdout**, and **stderr** are special cases of files processed by high-level processing. Use of these files is collectively referred to as *standard input and output* and requires the inclusion of **stdio.h**. The relationship between the three files and the two levels of I/O processing is summarized in Figure 4.2.

	High Level File Pointer	Low Level File descriptor
standard input	stdin	0
standard output	stdout	1
standard error	stderr	2

Figure 4.2 stdio and its relationship to file processing

Before **main( )** is entered during program execution, these three, text-only files are automatically opened by the compiler for high-level, file I/O. Thus, the files are unique in that they do not have to be explicitly opened by a program. In addition, their file pointers are compiler constants, defined in **stdio.h**, where the values of other, high-level file pointers are variable values assigned at file-open time. Their associated file pointers are symbolically referred to as **stdin**, **stdout**, and **stderr**.

Data written to both **stdout** and **stderr** normally appear on the terminal display. Data arriving on **stdin** normally arrive from the keyboard. Note that EOF can often be signaled from the keyboard as a **control-keystroke (ctrl-z, ctrl-d, etc.)**.

On some systems, these three files possibly consume three system file control blocks, diminishing the number of file-control blocks available for other file processing.

Redirection

UNIX is able to automatically divert the **stdin** and **stdout** data streams. This process, called **I/O redirection**, allows **stdin** data to originate from devices and data files instead of from the keyboard. Likewise, redirection allows **stdout** data that would normally appear on your display to be placed in a dataset or on another device. The data may be placed in a new dataset or be appended to an existing one.

Redirection is not detectable by an executing program and is so useful it has been implemented by several C compilers that do not operate in a UNIX environment. Note that redirection is a UNIX characteristic that has been extended to C compilers. It is not part of the C language.

The variations of redirection are as follows:

To redirect **stdin**, invoke the desired program normally and append an extra parameter on the command line that names the desired input file preceded by a < as shown in Figure 4.3.

```
test1 parm-1 parm-2....parm-n <input.txt
```

Figure 4.3 stdin file redirection

Note that successful use of **stdin** redirection can be difficult with highly interactive programs.

To redirect **stdout** to a new data file, invoke the desired program normally and append an extra parameter on the command line that names the desired output file preceded by a > as shown in Figure 4.4.

```
test1 parm-1 parm-2....parm-n >output.txt
```

Figure 4.4 Creating a new file from redirected stdout output

To append redirected **stdout** output to a possibly existing data file, invoke the desired program normally and append an extra parameter on the command line that names the desired output data file preceded by a >> as shown in Figure 4.5.

```
test1 parm-1 parm-2....parm-n >>output.txt
```

Figure 4.5 Appending redirected stdout output to a file

If necessary, both **stdin** and **stdout** can be redirected on the same command line. The order of the redirection file parameters does not matter. That is:

```
test1 >outfile.txt <infile.txt
```

is equivalent to:

```
test1 <infile.txt  >outfile.txt
```

Under some UNIX shells, the command line directive:

```
2>filename
```

redirects **stderr** to a file (where 2 is the file descriptor of **stderr**). Note that **stderr** is generally not redirectable from the command line on non-UNIX systems. This insures that error messages will always appear on your terminal screen, (regardless of whether **stdout** has been redirected) unless **stderr** is explicitly redirected internally by a program.

If you compiler does support I/O redirection, the I/O redirection specifications will not appear as one of the input arguments arriving in **main( )** (ie. one of the arguments commonly referred to as ***argv[n]**).

If your compiler does not explicitly support I/O redirection, the redirection parameters will arrive as arguments in **main( )**. The program can then simulate I/O redirection under program control. This requires the use of the **freopen** function.

Piping

One final variation of I/O redirection is called **piping**. In this variant, the **stdout** data stream of one program is automatically fed to another program's **stdin**. The operating system may automatically place a system-dependent **EOF** at the end of the data. While piping is a UNIX feature and not a property of C, it is now appearing as a feature of other operating systems. It is triggered by using the piping symbol, as illustrated in Figure 4.6.

```
program1 <infile.txt | program2 | program3 >outfile.txt
```

Notes: Program1's stdout is program2's stdin. Program2's stdout is program3's stdin. Program1's stdin and program3's stdout are redirected.

Figure 4.6 Piping combined with I/O redirection

Figure 4.7 shows the hierarchy of file I/O functions.

High-Level (Buffered) I/O Functions

In high-level I/O, files are viewed as streams, which are described by structures. All high-level requests involve a file pointer that points to a file structure. In some environments, high-level I/O can only process text files. High-level processing requires the inclusion of **stdio.h**.

Processing Level	Associated Library Functions	Notes
High Level	fopen/freopen fclose fflush unlink fseek ftell fgetc/getc/getchar ungetc fputc/putc/putchar fgets/gets fputs/puts fread fwrite fprintf/printf/sprintf fscanf/scanf/sscanf feof ferror	Buffered Uses file descriptors Maybe text files only
Low Level	open close creat read write lseek tell	Unbuffered Uses file pointers Text and binary files
Operating System	Physical I/O Device Control	

Figure 4.7 Hierarchy of file I/O functions

A rule of thumb for high-level I/O might be:

```
To read/write a character, use getc/putc
To read/write a "word", use scanf/printf
To read/write a "line", use gets/puts
```

An end-of-file (EOF) terminates each file, but may vary in format from system to system. Be sure to use the symbolic EOF definition that usually is in each compiler's **stdio.h**. This will avoid system dependencies.

Figure 4.8 shows an example of high-level file handling.

```
#include "stdio.h"

char  mode1[] = "r";           /* "r"==>read; "w"==>write; "a"==>append */
char  mode2[] = "w";
char  file1[] = "in";
char  file2[] = "out";

main()
{
 FILE *fopen(), *file_ptr1, *file_ptr2; /* high level==>file pointers */

  int   c;

    file_ptr1 = fopen(file1, mode1);  /* HAZARD - mode must be a STRING */
    file_ptr2 = fopen(file2, mode2);  /* HAZARD - mode must be a STRING */

    if ( (!file_ptr1) || (!file_ptr2) ) {
       abort("Can't open a file....");
    }

    while ( (c = getc(file_ptr1)) != EOF )       /* advances file position */
       putc(c, file_ptr2);

    fclose(file_ptr1);                      /* read-only ==> flushes the buffer */
    fclose(file_ptr2);   /* flushes the buffer and might update directory */

}
```

Figure 4.8 High level file handling example

Low-Level (UNIX) I/O Functions

In low-level I/O, all requests involve integer file descriptors that are used by the operating system. All low-level requests result in calls to the operating system, which may or may not have the data in buffers.

Figure 4.9 shows an example of low-level (UNIX) file handling.

```
#define INPUT   0
#define OUTPUT  1
#define BOTH    2

char InputFile[]  = "in";
char OutputFile[] = "out";

main()
{
  int   InFile,  OutFile;
  long  lseek(), length;
  int   c;


  InFile  = open(InputFile , INPUT);
  OutFile = creat(OutputFile, OUTPUT);

  printf("\nInfile  = %d", InFile);
  printf("\nOutfile = %d", OutFile);

  if ((InFile < 0) || (OutFile < 0))
     abort("Files cannot be opened...");

  printf("\nSize of input file is %ld.", lseek(InFile, 0L, 2));

  lseek(InFile, 0L, 0);                         /*reset to beginning */

  while (read(InFile,&c,1) != 0)                /* read a character  */
        write(OutFile, &c, 1);                  /* write a character */

  c = 26;
  write(OutFile, &c, 1);                        /* write an EOF for PC/DOS */

  close(InFile);
  close(OutFile);

}
```

Figure 4.9 Low-level (UNIX) file handling example

Understanding Library Function Descriptions

In each of the following library function descriptions, the function's argument declarations are described as they would be in the library. Note that some, such as **fseek**, require that the arguments are **long**. This can be accomplished by using the cast operator or by using the X3J11 function prototype declaration.

fclose

```
int fclose(file_ptr)
FILE *file_ptr;
```

The **fclose** Function closes a file opened for high-level processing after flushing any buffered output data. If successful, a zero is returned. Otherwise an **EOF** is returned.

feof

```
int feof(file_ptr)
FILE *file_ptr;
```

The **feof** Function tests for an end-of-file condition on the file associated with **file_ptr**. **feof** returns a non-zero value if an end-of-file condition exists for the file. Otherwise it returns a zero value.

ferror

```
int ferror(file_ptr)
FILE *file_ptr;
```

The **ferror** Function returns a non-zero value if the file associated with **file_ptr** has experienced an error. The error indication will continue until it is cleared by a **clearerr(file_ptr)** call, or until the file is closed.

fflush

```
int fflush(file_ptr)
FILE *file_ptr;
```

The **fflush** Function writes all buffered output data to the appropriate file. In contrast to the **fclose** Function, the file remains open. If successful, a zero is returned. Otherwise an **EOF** is returned. If **fflush** is used on an input-only file, the call is ignored.

fgetc/getc/getchar

```
int fgetc(file_ptr)                          /* a general file */
FILE *file_ptr;

#define getc(file_ptr) fgetc(file_ptr)       /* a general file */
#define getchar() fgetc(stdin)               /* stdin only     */
```

The **fgetc** Function returns the next character from the file or an **EOF** at the end-of-file. The receiving variable should be declared an **int** so EOF can be distinguished from any character value.

The **getc** and **getchar** Functions are macros that may cause side effects.

fgets

```
char *fgets(buffer, buffer_length, file_ptr)
char buffer[];
int  buffer_length;
FILE *file_ptr;
```

The **fgets** Function reads data from a file until a newline is encountered, the buffer is filled (includes a compiler-appended null), or an end-of-file is reached. The data are always appended with a compiler-generated null, which determines the length of the received data. If the input is terminated by a newline, the newline is included in the returned string as well. **fgets** returns a pointer to the input buffer and a **NULL** if an error occurs or an end-of-file is reached. A suitable invocation would be of the form:

```
if (fgets(buffer,buffer_length,file_ptr) == (char *) NULL) ...
```

fopen/freopen

```
FILE *fopen(file_name, file_mode)              /* high-level I/O */
char file_name[], file_mode[];

FILE *freopen(file_name, file_mode, file_ptr)  /* redirection function */
char file_name[], file_mode[];
FILE *file_ptr;
```

1981

Sun's FOPEN(3S) says an fseek, rewind, or reading EOF is required before switching between reading and writing a "+" mode stream; and that the "+" mode is "unrel

The **fopen** Function opens the file indicated in the first parameter for high-level processing in the mode indicated by the second parameter. If successful, it returns a file descriptor; otherwise it returns a null pointer. See Figure 4.10 for a summary of the values for mode. Note that both parameters are strings and that the file mode specification is not a character. Moreover, note that using a mode of **a** or **a+** prevents a program from writing anywhere except at the end of the file even if it seeks into the middle of the file.

The **freopen** Function closes the file currently associated with **file__ptr**. It then reopens it in the new **file__mode** and associated with the new **file__name**. The file pointer value does not change. This function is typically used by programs to redirect the standard input and output files that have compiler-constant file pointer values.

Note:

The **mode** may have a **b** appended to indicate that the file is a binary file vs. a text file.

Mode	Means	File Exists	File Does Not Exist
"r"	Read Only	OK	ERROR
"r+"	Read and Write	OK	ERROR
"w"	Write Only	Erases Old File	Creates New File
"w+"	Read and Write	Erases Old File	Creates New File
"a"	Append	Appends To Old File	Creates New File
"a+"	Read and Write	Appends To Old File	Creates New File

Figure 4.10 fopen mode summary

fprintf/printf/sprintf

```
int fprintf(file_ptr, control_string, arguments)    /* to a file */
FILE *file_ptr
char control_string[];

int printf(control_string, arguments)               /* to stdout */
char control_string[];

int sprintf(buffer, control_string, arguments)      /* to memory */
char buffer[], control_string[];
```

The **fprintf** Function places formatted output to the file associated with **file__ptr**. The output is formatted under control of the control string. The control string is described in *The printf Control String*. **fprintf** returns an **EOF** in the event of an error.

The **printf** Function is equivalent to **fprintf** except that the I/O is directed to **stdout**.

The **sprintf** Function is equivalent to **fprintf** except that the formatted output is placed in a memory buffer and terminated with a **NUL**. No string-overflow checking is done.

fputc/putc/putchar

```
int fputc(c, file_ptr)                          /* to a general file */
char c;
FILE *file_ptr;

#define putc(c, file_ptr) fputc(c, file_ptr)    /* to a general file */

#define putchar(c)        fputc(c, stdout)       /* to stdout          */
```

The **fputc** Function appends the designated character to the appropriate file. It returns the appended character if successful or an **EOF** in the event of an error.

The **putc** Function and the **putchar** Function are macros that may cause side effects.

fputs/puts

```
int fputs(buffer, file_ptr)                     /* to a general file */
char buffer[];
FILE *file_ptr;

int puts(buffer)                                /* to stdout          */
char buffer[];
```

The **fputs** Function copies a null-terminated string to the file associated with **file_ptr**. **puts** copies the string with an appended **newline** to **stdout**. **fputs( )** does not append a **newline**. In neither case does the string's terminating NUL get copied to the file. Both routines return an **EOF** in the event of an error.

Alternately, **puts** may be defined as follows:

```
#define puts(buffer) fputs(buffer,stdout)
```

fread

```
int fread(buffer, size, count, file_ptr)
char buffer[];
int  size;
int  count;
FILE *file_ptr;
```

The **fread** Function attempts to read **count** occurrences of objects, each of size **size** into **buffer** from the file associated with the file descriptor **fd**.

The **fread** Function returns the number of objects successfully read.

fscanf/scanf/sscanf

```
int fscanf(file_ptr, control_string, pointer_arguments)    /* from a file */
FILE *file_ptr
char control_string[];

int scanf(control_string, pointer_arguments)               /* from stdin */
char control_string[];                                     /* '\n' unread */

int sscanf(buffer, control_string, pointer_arguments)      /* from memory */
char buffer[], control_string[];
```

The **fscanf** Function reads characters from the files associated with **file__ptr** and interprets them according to the accompanying **control__string**. The resulting values are stored in the locations indicated by the accompanying pointer values. The control string is described in *The scanf Control String*. **scanf** returns an integer, which indicates the number of successfully matched items. In contrast to **fgets**, terminating newlines are left unread and must be discarded with a subsequent **getchar** invocation.

The **scanf** Function is similar to **fscanf** except that the input always comes from **stdin**.

The **sscanf** Function is similar to **fscanf** except that the input comes from a string in memory.

Hazard:

These functions require pointers for successful storage of converted data. This requires prepending an address operator to the identifier of objects to receive the converted values, *except for strings*.

fseek

```
int fseek(file_ptr, offset, base)
FILE *file_ptr;
long offset;                              /* HAZARD - long */
int base;
```

The **fseek** Function flushes the high-level I/O buffer(s) and repositions the file read/write pointer. This effectively extends low-level, random-processing capability to a file opened for high-level I/O. The only portable way to use **fseek** is with values that have been returned by **ftell** or by insuring that the second argument (offset) is zero.

The allowed values for **base** are:

```
0   Relative to the beginning of the file
1   Relative to the current read/write file position
2   Relative to the end of the file
```

The value of **offset** is added to **base** to calculate the target position.

The **fseek** Function returns a zero if successful and a non-zero value if unsuccessful.

ftell

```
long ftell(file_ptr)
FILE *file_ptr;
```

The **ftell** Function returns the current value of the read/write position pointer for a file. The value is the distance of the pointer's position from the beginning of the file, expressed in terms of characters. **ftell** returns a −1 if an error occurs.

fwrite

```
int fwrite(buffer, size, count, file_ptr)
char buffer[];
int   size;
int   count;
FILE *file_ptr;
```

The **fwrite** Function attempts to write **count** occurrences of objects, each of size **size** from **buffer** into the file associated with the file descriptor **fd**.

fwrite returns the number of objects successfully written.

gets

```
(char *) gets(buffer)
char buffer[];
```

The **gets** Function reads data from **stdin** until a **newline** is encountered. The **newline** is discarded and the data is always appended with a compiler-generated NUL, which determines the length of the received data. **gets** returns a pointer to the input buffer.

The **gets** Function returns a **NULL** in the event of an error or end-of-file.

ungetc

```
int ungetc(c, file_ptr)
char c;
FILE *file_ptr;
```

The **ungetc** Function pushes the character c back into the open input file for subsequent processing later. Only one character may be pushed back at any given time for a file. **ungetc** returns a zero if successful, a − 1 if not.

unlink

```
int unlink(file_name)
char file_name[];
```

The **unlink** Function erases a file from the system. It returns a zero if successful, a − 1 if not. Depending on the implementation, the file may or may not have to be closed.

Low-Level (Unbuffered) I/O

Low-level file I/O attempts to emulate UNIX's view of a file system. Open files are uniquely identified by numeric values, called **file descriptors**. For some systems, low-level file I/O is the only mechanism for writing binary files from C programs.

close

```
int close(fd)
int fd;
```

The **close** Function closes the file associated with the file descriptor **fd**. It returns a zero if successful, a − 1 if not.

creat

```
int creat(file_name, mode)
char *file_name;
char mode;
```

The **creat** Function creates a new file or erases an old one in order to create a new file with the same name as the old one. The values of **mode** vary so widely from compiler to compiler, they do not bear discussion.

The **creat** Function returns a zero if successful, a −1 if not.

lseek

```
long lseek( fd, offset, base)
int fd;
long offset;
int base;
```

The **lseek** Function moves the read/write pointer for the file associated with the file descriptor **fd**.

The allowed values for base are:

```
0   Relative to the beginning of the file
1   Relative to the current read/write file position
2   Relative to the end of the file
```

The value of **offset** is added to base to calculate the target position.

The **lseek** Function returns the value of the file's read/write pointer if successful and a −1 if unsuccessful.

open

```
int open(file_name, mode)
char *file_name;
char mode;
```

The **open** Function opens an existing file for reading or writing. The values of **mode** vary widely from compiler to compiler. In UNIX, they have the following meaning:

Value	Meaning
0	input
1	output
2	both

Other values may be included as well.

The **open** Function returns a zero if successful, a −1 if not.

read

```
int read(fd, buffer, count)
int fd;
char     buffer[];
unsigned count;
```

The **read** Function attempts to read **count** bytes from the file associated with the file descriptor **fd** into the buffer **buffer**. The read begins at the position indicated by the file's read/write pointer. When the read is complete, the file read/write pointer is advanced by the number of successfully read bytes.

The **read** Function returns the number of successfully read bytes. This number may be less than the number of characters requested. If an end of file is reached, a value of zero is returned. If an error is detected, a −1 is returned.

tell

```
#define tell(fd) lseek(fd, (long) 0, 1)
```

Sun manual, 1983, says obsolete

The **tell** Function is not implemented on all systems but may be emulated with a macro. **tell** returns the current position of the file associated with the file descriptor. The value is presented as a **long** value.

write

```
int write(fd, buffer, count)
int fd;
char    buffer[];
unsigned count;
```

The **write** Function attempts to write **count** bytes to the file associated with the file descriptor **fd** from the buffer **buffer**. The write begins at the position indicated by the file's read/write pointer. When the write is complete, the file read/write pointer is advanced by the number of successfully written bytes.

The **write** Function returns the number of successfully written bytes. This may be less than the number of characters requested, in which case there is an error. If an end-of-file is reached, a value of zero is returned. If an error is detected and no characters can be written to the file, a −1 is returned.

The printf Control String

The **fprintf**, **printf**, and **sprintf** functions all use the same format-control string. The control string can be dynamically built in a character array rather than being coded in the function call since the functions only receive a pointer to the control string.

The conversion characters are illustrated in Figure 4.11. Remember that all arguments are subject to promotion. Thus all **char** values are promoted to **int**s and *all float values are promoted to double*.

Conv. Char(s)	Valid Object Type	Produces	Example
%c	char	single character	(a)
%s	string	zero or more chars, NUL terminated	(hello)
%d	int	signed decimal integer	(-976)
%o	int	unsigned octal integer	(2760)
%u	unsigned	unsigned decimal integer	(1520)
%x	int	unsigned hex. integer, uses a-f	(5f0)
%X	int	unsigned hex. integer, uses A-F	(5F0)
%ld	long	signed decimal integer	(-9999999)
%lo	long	unsigned long octal integer	(1553433)
%lu	unsigned long	unsigned decimal integer	(4487283)
%lx	long	unsigned long hex. integer, uses a-f	(6d71b)
%lX	long	unsigned long hex. integer, uses A-F	(6D71B)
%f	float/double	[-]ddd.dddddd, six places max	(14.883265)
%e	float/double	[-]d.dddddde[s]dd*, six places max	(1.724322e-14)
%E	float/double	[-]d.dddddE[s]dd*, six places max	(1.724322E-14)
%g	float/double	real number, shorter of %f or %e	
%G	float/double	real number, shorter of %F or %E	
%Lf	long double	[-]ddd.dddddd,	(14.883265)
%Le	long double	[-]d.dddddde[s]dd*	(1.724322e-14)
%LE	long double	[-]d.dddddE[s]dd*	(1.724322E-14)
%Lg	long double	real number, shorter of %Lf or %Le	
%LG	long double	real number, shorter of %LF or %LE	
%%	n/a	a single percent sign	(%)

*s stands for a plus or minus sign

Figure 4.11 fprint/printf/sprintf conversion characters

The control characters may be further qualified by one or more **flag** characters, a **field width** specification, and a **precision** specification as shown in Figure 4.12.

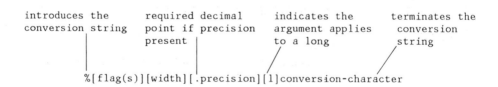

```
introduces the      required decimal    indicates the       terminates the
conversion string   point if precision   argument applies    conversion
                    present              to a long           string
         |            |                      /                  /
%[flag(s)][width][.precision][l]conversion-character
```

Figure 4.12 Qualification of printf conversion characters by optional flag characters, width specification, and precision specification

The flag characters are described in Figure 4.13.

The field width is an optional specification that indicates the **minimum** number of positions used to present the value. If the value requires more positions, they will be used. If the value can be presented in fewer positions, it will be padded on the left or right, depending on whether or not it is right justified (the default) or left-justified (indicated by a flag character) respectively. The padding character is selected by a flag character; it defaults to zeros for numbers and spaces for strings and characters. Characters and strings can never be zero-padded. The field width can be specified by either a decimal-digit string or an asterisk, in which case the value for the field width is understood to be the next, argument in the argument list.

flag char.	Description
-	The value is left justified within its field.
+	The value will always be preceded by a plus or minus sign.
space	Nonnegative values will always be preceded by spaces.
#	1) Ignored for %c, %s, %d, %u, %ld, and %lu conversions. 2) For %o and %lo conversions, the field width is extended to include to include a leading zero. 3) For %x, %lx, %X, and %lX conversions, the field width is extended to include a 0x, 0x, 0X, and 0X respectively. 4) For %e, %E, %f, %g, and %G conversions, the converted value will always contain a decimal point. 5) In the case of %g and %G, zeros trailing the decimal point are not removed.

Figure 4.13 printf flag characters

A decimal point signals an optional precision specification. If a decimal point is not followed by a decimal-digit string or an asterisk, the precision defaults to zero. The precision is interpreted as follows:

For a %s conversion, it specifies the **maximum** number of characters to present.

For %d, %o, %u, %x, %X, %ld, %lo, %lu, %lx, and %1X conversions, it specifies the **minimum** number of digits to present.

For %e, %E, and %f conversions, it specifies the number of digits to present after the decimal point.

For %g and %G conversions, it specifies the **maximum** number of significant digits to present.

The precision can be specified by either a decimal-digit string or an asterisk, in which case the value for the precision is understood to be the next argument in the argument list.

The scanf Control String

The **fscanf**, **scanf**, and **sscanf** functions all use the same control string conversion-specification format illustrated in Figure 4.14. These control strings may contain:

Conversion specifications or, alternately, an asterisk that consumes the appropriate number of stream characters, but suppresses the assignment of the produced value to the target object.

Ordinary characters (excluding the percent sign) that must match the current input character in the stream.

Whitespace, which causes all whitespace to be discarded in the stream up to the next, non-whitespace character.

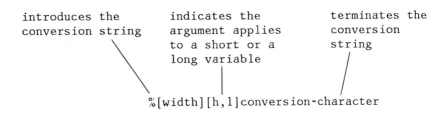

Figure 4.14 Format of the fscanf/scanf/sscanf conversion specifications

Because the functions receive a pointer to the control string, the control string can be dynamically built in a character array instead of being coded in the statement. The remaining arguments are pointers to objects to receive the converted data. This often is an object name preceded by a **&**. The **&** is not needed in the case of character arrays.

The optional field-width specifier is used to limit the number of input characters consumed in the individual conversion processes.

The conversion characters and their modifiers are illustrated in Figure 4.15.

The functions terminate when the control string is consumed, at an end of file, or when an illegal character is detected. The functions all return a count of the successful conversions to the calling function, unless an end-of-file is detected, in which case an **EOF** is returned.

Hazard:

In the event of an illegal character, the offending character remains in the stream and will be the first character accessed in the next file read.

Target Object	Conv. Char(s)	Comments
char	%c	Single char input, possibly whitespace if there are no intervening spaces between the %c and the preceding specification.
short	%hd %ho %hx	[-]ddddd input format. Octal input format. Hexadecimal input format.
int	%d %o %x	[-]ddddd input format. Octal input format. Hexadecimal input format.
long	%D, %ld, %lD %O, %lo, %lO %X, %lx, %lX	[-]ddddd input format. Octal input format. Hexadecimal input format.
float	%e, %f	[-]dddd.dddd or [-]d.dddde[s*]dd input format.
double	%le, %lf, %E, %F	[-]dddd.dddd or [-]d.dddde[s*]dd input format.
long double	%Le, %Lf, %LE, %LF	[-]dddd.dddd or [-]d.dddde[s*]dd input format.
char array	%nc	Character input; n is a field-width specifier. n characters are read and placed in the character array. No null terminator is generated.
string	%s	String input. Begins with first non-whitespace character and ends with the first whitespace character. The produced string is NULL terminated. If a field width modifier is present, then the indicated number of characters is read, provided a whitespace character is not encountered first.
	[....]	String input not delimited by whitespace. If the first character within the brackets is the character '¬', then the subsequent characters listed within the brackets are the only characters that will terminate the string. If the first character within the brackets is not the character '¬', then the characters listed within the string are the only characters that are considered valid. Any other character within the stream will terminate the individual conversion process. This type conversion process allows whitespace to be imbedded within converted strings. The terminating character is left in the stream. The string is NULL terminated.

*s stands for a plus or minus sign

Figure 4.15 fscanf/scanf/sscanf conversion characters

Appendixes

- **ASCII Character Set**
- **The ctype.h Header**
- **Operator Precedence Table**
- **High-Level and Low-Level I/O Functions**
- **Sample Library Reference Summary**
- **printf/scanf Control String Formats**
- **C Language Summary**

ASCII
Character Set

char	key	dec.	octal	hex	class	char	dec.	octal	hex	class
NUL	^@	0	\000	\x00	c	' '	32	\040	\x20	pvw
SOH	^A	1	\001	\x01	c	'!'	33	\041	\x21	pv
STX	^B	2	\002	\x02	c	'"'	34	\042	\x22	pv
ETX	^C	3	\003	\x03	c	'#'	35	\043	\x23	pv
EOT	^D	4	\004	\x04	c	'$'	36	\044	\x24	pv
ENQ	^E	5	\005	\x05	c	'%'	37	\045	\x25	pv
ACK	^F	6	\006	\x06	c	'&'	38	\046	\x26	pv
BEL	^G	7	\007	\x07	c	'''	39	\047	\x27	pv
BS	^H	8	\010	\x08	c	'('	40	\050	\x28	pv
TAB	^I	9	\011	\x09	cw	')'	41	\051	\x29	pv
LF	^J	10	\012	\x0A	cw	'*'	42	\052	\x2A	pv
VT	^K	11	\013	\x0B	cw	'+'	43	\053	\x2B	pv
FF	^L	12	\014	\x0C	cw	','	44	\054	\x2C	pv
CR	^M	13	\015	\x0D	cw	'-'	45	\055	\x2D	pv
SO	^N	14	\016	\x0E	c	'.'	46	\056	\x2E	pv
SI	^O	15	\017	\x0F	c	'/'	47	\057	\x2F	pv
DLE	^P	16	\020	\x10	c	'0'	48	\060	\x30	bdv
DC1	^Q	17	\021	\x11	c	'1'	49	\061	\x31	bdv
DC2	^R	18	\022	\x12	c	'2'	50	\062	\x32	bdv
DC3	^S	19	\023	\x13	c	'3'	51	\063	\x33	bdv
DC4	^T	20	\024	\x14	c	'4'	52	\064	\x34	bdv
NAK	^U	21	\025	\x15	c	'5'	53	\065	\x35	bdv
SYN	^V	22	\026	\x16	c	'6'	54	\066	\x36	bdv
ETB	^W	23	\027	\x17	c	'7'	55	\067	\x37	bdv
CAN	^X	24	\030	\x18	c	'8'	56	\070	\x38	bdv
EM	^Y	25	\031	\x19	c	'9'	57	\071	\x39	bdv
SUB	^Z	26	\032	\x1A	c	':'	58	\072	\x3A	pv
ESC	^[	27	\033	\x1B	c	';'	59	\073	\x3B	pv
FS	^\	28	\034	\x1C	c	'<'	60	\074	\x3C	pv
GS	^]	29	\035	\x1D	c	'='	61	\075	\x3D	pv
RS	^^	30	\036	\x1E	c	'>'	62	\076	\x3E	pv
US	^_	31	\037	\x1F	c	'?'	63	\077	\x3F	pv

char	dec.	octal	hex	class	char	dec.	octal	hex	class
'@'	64	\100	\x40	pv	'\`'	96	\140	\x60	pv
'A'	65	\101	\x41	abuv	'a'	97	\141	\x61	ablv
'B'	66	\102	\x42	abuv	'b'	98	\142	\x62	ablv
'C'	67	\103	\x43	abuv	'c'	99	\143	\x63	ablv
'D'	68	\104	\x44	abuv	'd'	100	\144	\x64	ablv
'E'	69	\105	\x45	abuv	'e'	101	\145	\x65	ablv
'F'	70	\106	\x46	abuv	'f'	102	\146	\x66	ablv
'G'	71	\107	\x47	abuv	'g'	103	\147	\x67	ablv
'H'	72	\110	\x48	abuv	'h'	104	\150	\x68	ablv
'I'	73	\111	\x49	abuv	'i'	105	\151	\x69	ablv
'J'	74	\112	\x4A	abuv	'j'	106	\152	\x6A	ablv
'K'	75	\113	\x4B	abuv	'k'	107	\153	\x6B	ablv
'L'	76	\114	\x4C	abuv	'l'	108	\154	\x6C	ablv
'M'	77	\115	\x4D	abuv	'm'	109	\155	\x6D	ablv
'N'	78	\116	\x4E	abuv	'n'	110	\156	\x6E	ablv
'O'	79	\117	\x4F	abuv	'o'	111	\157	\x6F	ablv
'P'	80	\120	\x50	abuv	'p'	112	\160	\x70	ablv
'Q'	81	\121	\x51	abuv	'q'	113	\161	\x71	ablv
'R'	82	\122	\x52	abuv	'r'	114	\162	\x72	ablv
'S'	83	\123	\x53	abuv	's'	115	\163	\x73	ablv
'T'	84	\124	\x54	abuv	't'	116	\164	\x74	ablv
'U'	85	\125	\x55	abuv	'u'	117	\165	\x75	ablv
'V'	86	\126	\x56	abuv	'v'	118	\166	\x76	ablv
'W'	87	\127	\x57	abuv	'w'	119	\167	\x77	ablv
'X'	88	\130	\x58	abuv	'x'	120	\170	\x78	ablv
'Y'	89	\131	\x59	abuv	'y'	121	\171	\x79	ablv
'Z'	90	\132	\x5A	abuv	'z'	122	\172	\x7A	ablv
'['	91	\133	\x5B	pv	'{'	123	\173	\x7B	pv
'\'	92	\134	\x5C	pv	'|'	124	\174	\x7C	pv
']'	93	\135	\x5D	pv	'}'	125	\175	\x7D	pv
'^'	94	\136	\x5E	pv	'~'	126	\176	\x7E	pv
'_'	95	\137	\x5F	pv	del	127	\177	\x7F	c

class symbols

symbol	meaning
a	alphabetic
b	alphanumeric
c	control
d	digit
l	lower case
p	punctuation
u	upper case
v	printable
w	whitespace

The ctype.h
Header

The **ctype.h** header is a file that can be included in a program to facilitate character-type tests. The tests and their purposes are listed below. Appendix A lists the various characters and their types.

Test	Purpose
isalpha(ch)	Tests if ch is A-Z or a-z
isalnum(ch)	Tests if ch is A-Z, a-z, or 0-9
isascii(ch)	Tests if ch is an ASCII character
iscntrl(ch)	Tests if ch has a value between 0 to 32 or is 127
isdigit(ch)	Tests if ch is 0-9
islower(ch)	Tests if ch is a-z
isprint(ch)	Tests if ch is any printable character
ispunct(ch)	Tests if ch is a punctuation character
isspace(ch)	Tests if ch is blank, form feed, newline, space, or tab
isupper(ch)	Tests if ch is A-Z
isxdigit(ch)	Tests if character is 0-9, A-F, or a-f

Operator Precedence Table and C Keywords

class	operator name	operator	direction	precedence	
Primary Expression	Function call Array element Struct pointer Struct member	() [] -> . defined	——————►	1	HIGH
Unary	Auto-PostInc. Auto-PostDec.	++ --	——————►	2	
	Logical inverse Ones complement Negation Unary Plus Pointer Auto-Preinc. Auto-Predec. Address Cast	! ○ - + * ++ -- & (type) sizeof	◄——————		
Multiplicative	Multiplication Division Modulus	* / %	——————►	3	
Additive		+ -	——————►	4	
Bitwise Shift	Shift left Shift right	<< >>	——————►	5	
Relational		< <= > >=	——————►	6	
Equality		== !=	——————►	7	

continued

Appendix C

173

class	operator name	operator	direction	precedence	
Bitwise	AND	&	⟶	8	↑
	Exclusive OR	⌃	⟶	9	
	Inclusive OR	|	⟶	10	
Logical Connective	Logical AND	&&	⟶	11	
	Logical OR	||	⟶	12	
Ternary	Conditional	? :	⟵	13	
Assignment	Shift Bitwise Bitwise	= %= += -= *= /= >>= <<= &= ⌃= |=	⟵	14	
	comma	,	⟶	15	LOW

High-Level and Low-Level I/O Functions

High Level I/O Functions

```
int fclose(file_ptr)
int feof(file_ptr)
int ferror(file_ptr)
int fflush(file_ptr)
int fgetc(file_ptr)                                    /* a general file    */
char *fgets(buffer, buffer_length, file_ptr)
FILE *fopen(file_name, file_mode)                      /* high-level I/O     */
FILE *freopen(file_name, file_mode, file_ptr)    /* redirection        */
int fprintf(file_ptr, control_string, arguments) /* to a file          */
int printf(file_ptr, control_string, arguments)  /* to  stdout         */
int sprintf(file_ptr, control_string, arguments) /* to memory          */
int fputc(c, file_ptr)                                 /* to a general file */
int puts(buffer)                                       /* to stdout          */
int fputs(buffer, file_ptr)                            /* to a general file */
int fread(buffer, size, count, file_ptr)
int fscanf(file_ptr, control_string, pointer_arguments)    /* from a file  */
int scanf(control_string, pointer_arguments)               /* from stdin   */
int sscanf(buffer, control_string, pointer_arguments)      /* from memory  */
int fseek(file_ptr, offset, base)
long ftell(file_ptr)
int fwrite(buffer, size, count, file_ptr)
(char *) gets(buffer)
int ungetc(c, file_ptr)
unlink(file_name)
#define getc(file_ptr) fgetc(file_ptr)                 /* a general file    */
#define getchar() fgetc(stdin)                         /* stdin only        */
#define putc(c, file_ptr) fputc(c, file_ptr)           /* to a general file */
#define putchar(c)        fputc(c, stdout)             /* to stdout          */
#define puts(buffer) fgets(buffer,stdout)              /* macro alternate    */
```

Low Level I/O Functions

```
int close(fd)
int creat(file_name, mode)
long lseek( fd, offset, base)
int open(file_name, mode)
int read(fd, buffer, count)
int write(fd, buffer, count)
#define tell(fd) lseek(fd, (long) 0, 1)
```

Sample Library Reference Summary

The following library functions are primarily extracted from the Microsoft™ C Version 3.0 Library Reference. The list is supplemented with functions from the X3J11 draft standard. Each actual parameter is cast to the correct type for reference.

```
void      abort();                                   /* terminate program  */
int       abs((int) n);                              /* absolute value int */
int       access((char *) pathname, (int) mode);     /* file check         */
double    acos((double) r);                          /* arc cosine of r    */
char      *asctime((struct tm *) time);              /* string time of day */
double    asin((double) r);                          /* arc sine of r      */
void      assert(expression);                        /* find logic errors  */
double    atan((double) x);                          /* arc tangent of x   */
double    atan2((double) x, (double) y);             /* arc tangent of x/y */
double    atof((char *) string);                     /* string to double   */
int       atoi((char *) string);                     /* string to integer  */
long      atol((char *) string);                     /* string to long     */

int       bdos((int) dosfn, (unsigned) dosdx,\       /* DOS function call  */
               (unsigned) dosal);

char      *bsearch((char *) key, (char *) base,\     /* array element query */
                   (unsigned) num, (unsigned) width,\
                   (int(* compare)()) );

double    cabs((struct complex) z);                  /* complex absolute value */
char      *calloc((unsigned) n, (unsigned) size);    /* allocate cleared array */
double    ceil((double) x);                          /* least int >= x     */
char      *cgets((char *) string);                   /* read console string */
int       chdir((char *) pathname);                  /* change directory   */
int       chmod((char *) pathname, (int) pmode);     /* change permission  */
int       chsize((int) handle, (long) size);         /* truncate file      */
void      clearerr((FILE *) stream);                 /* reset error/eof flag */
clock_t   clock();                                   /* time delta (ticks) */
int       close((int) handle);                       /* low-level file close */
double    cos((double) r);                           /* cosine of r        */
double    cosh((double) x);                          /* hyperbolic cosine of x */
int       cprintf((char *) format-string [,arg0, ...]); /* print on console*/
void      cputs((char *) string);                    /* console string write */
int       creat((char *) pathname, (int) pmode);     /* low-level file create */

int       cscanf((char *) format-string\             /* console read       */
                 [, (type *) arg0, ...]);

char      *ctime((long *) time);                     /* builds time string */
double    difftime((time_t) time2, (time_t) time1);  /* time delta (seconds)*/
```

```
int       dosexterr((struct DOSERROR *) buffer);  /* obtain DOS error      */
int       dup((int) handle);                       /* obtain second handle  */
int       dup2((int) handle1, (int) handle2);      /* force second handle id */
char      *ecvt((double) value, (int) ndigits,\    /* float to string       */
             (int *) decptr, (int *) signptr);

int       eof((int) handle);                       /* test for eof          */

int       execl((char *) pathname, (char *) arg0, ...,\    /* start child */
             (char *) argn, NULL);

int       execle((char *) pathname, (char *) arg0, ...,\   /* start child */
             (char *) argn, NULL, (char *[]) envp);

int       execlp((char *) pathname, (char *) arg0, ...,\   /* start child */
             (char *) argn, NULL);

int       execv((char *) pathname, (char *[]) argv);       /* start child */

int       execve((char *) pathname, (char *[]) argv,\      /* start child */
             (char *[]) envp);

int       execvp((char *) pathname, (char *[]) argv);      /* start child */
void      exit((int) status);                      /* exit and flush      */
void      _exit((int) status);                     /* exit, no flush      */
double    exp((double) x);                         /* exponential function */
double    fabs((double) x);                        /* float absolute value */
int       fclose ((FILE *) stream);                /* high-level close    */
int       fcloseall();                             /* close all high-level */

char      *fcvt((double) value, (int) ndigits,\    /* float to string     */
             (int *) decptr, (int *) signptr);

FILE      *fdopen((int) handle, (char *) type);    /* open stream using handle */
int       feof((FILE *) stream);                   /* test for eof        */
int       ferror((FILE *) stream);                 /* test for I/O error  */
int       fflush((FILE *) stream);                 /* flush I/O buffer    */
int       fgetc((FILE  *) stream);                 /* get stream character */
int       fgetchar();                              /* get stdin character */

char      *fgets((char *) string, (int) n,\        /* stream string read  */
             (FILE *) stream);

long      filelength((int) handle);                /* fetch file length   */

int       fileno((FILE *) stream);                 /* return file handle  */
double    floor((double) x);                       /* max int <= x        */
int       flushall();                              /* flush all buffers   */
double    fmod((double) x, (double)y);             /* remainder of x/y    */
FILE      *fopen((char *) pathname, (char *) type); /* low-level open      */
unsigned  FP_OFF((char far *) longptr);            /* long pointer offset */
unsigned  FP_SEG((char far *) longptr);            /* long pointer segment */

int       fprintf((FILE *) stream,                 /* stdout print        */
             (char *) format-string [, arg0, ..., argn]);
```

```
int      fputc((int) c, (FILE *) stream);        /* char write to stream */
int      fputchar((int) c);                       /* char write to stdout */
int      fputs((char *) string, (FILE *) stream); /* string to stream    */

int      fread((char *) buffer, (int) size,\      /* read count items of  */
              (int) count, (FILE *) stream);      /* size from stream     */

void     free((char *) pointer);                  /* deallocate memory    */

FILE     *freopen((char *) pathname,\             /* file redirection     */
              (char *) type, (FILE *) stream);

double   frexp((double) x, (int *) expptr); /* binary scientific notation */

int      fscanf((FILE *) stream,\                 /* stream scanf         */
              (char *) format-string\
              [, (type *) arg0, ...]);

int      fseek((FILE *) stream, (long) offset,\   /* set file pointer     */
              (int) origin);

int      fstat((int) handle, (struct stat *) buffer); /* file status      */
long     ftell((FILE *) stream);                  /* fetch file pointer   */
void     ftime((struct timeb *) timeptr);         /* fetch time           */

int      fwrite((char *) buffer, (int) size,\     /* stream write         */
              (int) count, (FILE *) stream);

char     *gcvt((double) value, (int) ndec,        /* float to string      */
              (char *) buffer);

int      getc((FILE *) stream);                   /* get stream character */
int      getchar();                               /* get stdin character  */
int      getch();                                 /* console char, no echo*/
int      getche();                                /* console char, echo   */
char     *getcwd((char *) pathbuf, (int) n); /* fetch directory path name */
char     *getenv((char *) varname);        /* search environment table    */
int      getpid();                                /* fetch process id      */
char     *gets((char *) buffer);                  /* read stdin string     */
char     *getw((FILE *) stream);                  /* read int from stream  */
struct tm *gmtime((long *) time);                 /* calculate GMT         */
double   hypot((double) x, (double) y);           /* calculate hypotenuse  */
int      inp((unsigned) port);                    /* read a port           */

int      int86((int) intno, (union REGS *) inregs,\   /* engine interrupt  */
              (union REGS *) outregs );

int      int86x((int) intno, (union REGS *) inregs,\  /* engine interrupt  */
              (union REGS *) outregs, (struct SREGS *) segregs);

int      intdos((union REGS *) inregs,\           /* DOS interrupt        */
              (union REGS *) outregs);

int      intdosx((union REGS *) inregs,\          /* DOS interrupt        */
              (union REGS *) outregs, (struct SREGS *) segregs);
```

```
int       isalnum((int) c);                        /* a-z, A-Z, 0-9 ?   */
int       isalpha((int) c);                        /* a-z, A-Z ?        */
int       isascii((int) c);                        /* 0x00-0xFF ?       */
int       isatty((int) handle);                    /* character device ? */
int       iscntrl((int) c);                        /* control character? */
int       isdigit((int) c);                        /* 0-9 ?             */
int       isgraph((int) c);                        /* graphic character? */
int       islower((int) c);                        /* a-z ?             */
int       isprint((int) c);                        /* print  character? */
int       ispunct((int) c);                        /* punctuation ?     */
int       isspace((int) c);                        /* white-space ?     */
int       isupper((int) c);                        /* A-Z ?             */
int       isxdigit((int) c);                       /* 0-9, a-f, A-F ?   */

char    * itoa((int) value, (char *) string,\      /* integer to ASCII  */
             (int) radix);

double    j0((double) x);                           /* 1st Bessel, order 0 */
double    j1((double) x);                           /* 1st Bessel, order 1 */
double    jn((int) n, (double) x);                  /* 1st Bessel, order n */
int       kbhit();                                  /* keystroke waiting? */
int       kill((int) pid, (int) signal);           /* end signal to process */
long      labs((long) n);                           /* long absolute value */
double    ldexp((double) x, (int) exp);            /* base 2 exp -> decimal */
struct tm *localtime((long *) time);               /* calculate local time */

int       locking((int) handle, (int) mode,\       /* file lock/unlock  */
             (long) nbyte);

double    log((double) x);                          /* natural logarithm */
double    log10((double) x);                        /* base 10 logarithm */
void      longjump((jmp_buf) env, (int) value);    /* restore stack env. */

long      lseek((int) handle, (long) offset,\      /* move file pointer */
             (int) origin);

char    *ltoa((long) value, (char *) string,\      /* long to string    */
             (int) radix);

char    *malloc((unsigned) size);                   /* allocate memory   */
int       matherr((struct exception *) x);          /* math error type   */

char    *memccpy((char *) dest, (char *) src,\      /* memory copy       */
             (int) c, (unsigned) cnt);

char    *memchr((char *) buf, (int) c,\             /* memory search     */
             (unsigned) count);

int       memcmp((char *) buf1, (char *) buf2,\     /* memory compare    */
             (unsigned) cnt);

char    *memcpy((char *) dest, (char *) src,\       /* memory copy       */
             (unsigned) cnt);
```

```
char    *memset((char *) dest, (int) c,\        /* replicate char     */
            (unsigned) cnt);

int     mkdir((char *) pathname);               /* create directory   */
char    *mktemp((char *) template);             /* make unique filename */
double  modf((double) x, (double *) intptr);    /* dismantle float     */

void    movedata((int) srcseg, (int) srcoff,\   /* memory copy        */
            (int) destseg, (int) destoff,\
            (unsigned) nbytes);

onexit_t onexit((onexit_t) function);           /* call function on exit */

int     open((char *) pathname, (int) oflag\    /* low-level file open */
            [,(int) pmode]);

int     outp((unsigned) port, (int) value);     /* output to port     */
void    perror((char *) string);                /* print stderr errorno msg */
double  pow((double) x, (double) y);            /* x to the y power   */
int     printf((char *) format-string [,arg0, ...]); /* print on stdout    */
int     putc((int) c, (FILE *) stream);         /* char write to stream */
int     putchar((int) c);                       /* char write to stdout */
int     putch((int) c);                         /* char write to console*/
int     putenv((char *) envstring);             /* change envir. vars. */
int     puts((char *) string);                  /* stdio string write  */
int     putw((int) binint, (FILE *) stream);    /* int write to stream */

void    qsort((char *) base, (unsigned) num,    /* execute a quicksort */
            (unsigned) width, (int *()) compare);

int     rand();                                 /* pseudo-random generate */

int     read((int) handle, (char *) buffer,\    /* low-level file read */
            (unsigned int));

char    *realloc((char *) ptr, (unsigned) size); /* change allocation size */
int     remove((char *) pathname);              /* delete a file       */
int     rename((char *) newname, (char *) oldname);  /* rename a file */
int     rewind((FILE *) stream);                /* file pointer --> 0   */
int     rmdir((char *) pathname);               /* remove empty directory*/
char    *sbrk((int) incr);                      /* reset break value   */

int     scanf((char *) format-string,\          /* stdio read         */
            [, (type *) arg0, ...]);

void    segread((struct SREGS *) segregs);      /* intel seg reg fetch */
void    setbuf((FILE *) stream, (char *) ptr);  /* change buffer       */

void    setvbuf((FILE *) stream, (char *) ptr,\ /* change buffer       */
            (int) type, (int) size);

int     setjmp((jmp_buf) env);                  /* save stack environment*/
int     setmode((int) handle, (int) mode);      /* set file xlate mode  */
```

```
int      (*signal((int) sig, (int (*)()) func))((int)); /* select int. proc. */
double   sin((double) r);                          /* sine of r            */
double   sinh((double) x);                         /* hyperbolic sine of x */

int      sopen((char *) pathname, (int) oflag,\    /* open with sharing    */
             (int) shflag, (int) pmode);

int      spawnl((int) modeflag, (char *) pathname,\  /* start a child      */
             (char *) arg0, ... , (char *) argn, NULL);

int      spawnle((int) modeflag, (char *) pathname,\  /* start a child     */
             (char *) arg0, ... , (char *) argn, NULL, (char *[]) envp);

int      spawnlp((int) modeflag, (char *) pathname,\  /* start a child     */
             (char *) arg0, ... , (char *) argn, NULL);

int      spawnv((int) modeflag, (char *) pathname,\   /* start a child     */
             (char *[]) argv);

int      spawnve((int) modeflag, (char *) pathname,\  /* start a child     */
             (char *[]) argv, (char *[]) envp);

int      spawnvp((int) modeflag, (char *) pathname,\  /* start a child     */
             (char *[]) argv);

int      sprintf((char *) buffer, (char *) format-string\ /* memory printf */
             [,arg0, ...]);

double   sqrt((double) x):                         /* square root     */
void     srand((unsigned) seed);                   /* seed randomizer */

int      sscanf((char *) buffer, (char *) format-string /* memory scanf  */
             [, (type *) arg0, ...]);

int      stat((char *) pathname,\                  /* file/directory status */
             (struct stat *) buffer);

char     *strcat((char *) string1, (char *) string2); /* concatenation     */
char     *strchr((char *) string1, (int) c);       /* find first          */
int      *strcmp((char *) string1, (char *) string2); /* case compare      */
int      *strcmpi((char *) string1, (char *) string2);/* compare, no case  */
char     *strcpy((char *) string1, (char *) string2); /* copy 2 to 1       */
int      *strcspn((char *) string1, (char *) string2);/* first substring not*/
char     *strdup((char *) string);                 /* duplicate string    */
int       strlen((char *) string);                 /* length              */
char     *strlwr((char *) string);                 /* upper to lower      */

char     *strncat((char *) string1, (char *) string2,\ /* concatenation (n) */
             (unsigned) n);

int      *strncmp((char *) string1, (char *) string2,\ /* case compare  (n) */
             (unsigned) n);

char     *strncpy((char *) string1, (char *) string2,\ /* copy 2 to 1   (n) */
             (unsigned) n);
```

182

```
char     *strnset((char *) string1, (int) c,\          /* initialize    (n) */
             (unsigned) n);

char     *strpbrk((char *) string1, (char *) string2); /* find first        */
char     *strrchr((char *) string, (int) c);           /* find last c       */
char     *strrev((char *) string);                     /* reverse string    */
char     *strset((char *) string, (int) c);            /* initialize to c   */
char     *strspn((char *) string1, (char *) string2);  /* find first not in */
double    strtod((char *) nptr, (char **) endptr);     /* string to double  */

double    strtol((char *) nptr, (char **) endptr,\     /* string to long    */
             (int) base);

char     *strtok((char *) string1, (char *) string2);  /* tokenize 1 via 2  */
char     *strupr((char *) string);                     /* lower to upper    */
void      swab((char *) source, (char *) dest, (int) n); /* reverse bytes    */
int       system((char *) string);                     /* shell command     */
double    tan((double) r);                             /* tangent of r      */
double    tanh((double) x);                          /* hyperbolic tangent of x */
long      tell((int) handle);                          /* fetch file position*/
long      time((long *) timeptr);                      /*  seconds since 1970*/
FILE     *tmpfile();                                   /* create temp. file  */
char     *tmpnam((char *) string);                     /* get temp. file name*/
int       toascii((int) c);                            /* c --> to ASCII     */
int       tolower((int) c);                            /* to lower case      */
int       _tolower((int) c);                           /* force upper->lower */
int       toupper((int) c);                            /* to upper case      */
int       _toupper((int) c);                           /* force lower->upper */
void      tzset();                                     /* time zone set      */

char     *ultoa((unsigned long) value, (char *) string,\ /* convert to ASCII*/
             (int) radix);

int       unmask((int) pmode);                         /* set permission mask */
int       ungetc((int) c, (FILE *) stream);            /* put c back          */
int       ungetch((int) c);                            /* put c back console  */
int       unlink((char *) pathname);                   /* delete file         */

int       utime((char *) pathname,\                    /* set modification file time */
             (struct utimbuf *) times);

int       vfprintf((char *) format string, (va_list) arg); /* var. fprintf  */
int       vprintf((char *) format string, (va_list) arg);  /* var. printf   */

int       vsprintf((char *) buffer, (char *) format string,\ /* var. sprintf*/
             (va_list) arg);

int       write((int) handle, (char *) buffer,\        /* count bytes to handle */
             (unsigned) count );

double    y0((double) x);                              /* 2nd Bessel, order 0 */
double    y1((double) x);                              /* 2nd Bessel, order 1 */
double    yn((int) n, (double) x);                     /* 2nd Bessel, order n */
```

printf/scanf Control String Formats

printf conversion format

%[flag(s)][width][.precision][l,L]conversion-character

flag value	meaning
-	left justify within field
+	display sign of value
blank	if no sign, prepend a blank
#	octal => prepend a zero
	hex => prepend 0X or 0x
	real => display decimal point
	integer => no effect

width => minimum size of display field in characters
* => specified as next argument

type of conversion	precision meaning
integer	number of digits
real	digits after decimal point
string	number of characters

Conv. Char(s)	Valid Object Type	Conv. Char(s)	Valid Object Type
%c	char	%lX	long
%s	string	%f	float/double
%d	int	%e	float/double
%o	int	%E	float/double
%u	unsigned	%g	float/double
%x	int	%G	float/double
%X	int	%Lf	long double
%ld	long	%Le	long double
%lo	long	%LE	long double
%lu	unsigned long	%Lg	long double
%lx	long	%LG	long double

scanf conversion format

%[*][width][h,1,L]conversion-character

* => skip field

width => maximum size of field

Target Object	Conversion Character(s)
char	%c
short	%hd, %ho, %hx
int	%d, %o, %x
long	%D, %ld, %1D, %O, %lo, %lO, %X, %lx, %1X
float	%e, %f
double	%le, %lf, %E, %F
long double	%Le, %Lf,
char array	%nc
string	%s, [...], [¬...]

C Language Summary

Constants

Character : 'a'   '\0'   '0'   '\0227'   '\0x0D'

Escape sequences	
\a	sound alert
\b	backspace (BS)
\f	form feed (FF)
\n	newline (NL -or- LF)
\t	horizontal tab (HT)
\v	vertical tab
\r	carriage return (CR)
\(NL)	line continuation
\"	double quote (")
\'	single quote (')
\\	backslash (\)
\ddd	octal constant
\xddd	hexadecimal constant
\Xddd	hexadecimal constant

String: "\nThis is a character array"

Integer: 1520   -16   (decimal)
            1520L   -16L   (long)
            987654321   (long)
            0221   (octal)
            0221L   (long octal)
            0x2BAD   (hexadecimal)
            0x2BADL   (long hexadecimal)

Enumerated: {beans, pumpkins, squash, oranges}

Floating: 14.   14.1   14.1e0   14.1E+0
            .3   .3e-22 .3E-22   .3e+22
            12e-16 4e+12

Fundamental Data Types

```
Integer: signed char, unsigned char,  char
         signed int,   unsigned [int], int
         signed short [int], unsigned short [int], short [int]
         signed long [int],  unsigned long [int],  long [int]

Floating: float, double, long double

Object specification: [sscl] data-type object-name;
```

Object promotion and conversion

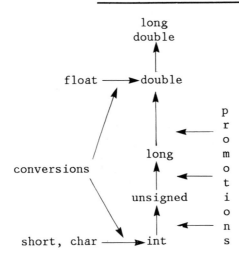

Storage Class, Initialization, and Visibility

Storage Class	Declared	Initialization	Visibility
auto	in fun.	any expression	local/block
register	in fun.	any expression	local/block
static	in fun. outside fun.	constant expr. constant expr.	local/block file
extern	in fun. outside fun.	illegal illegal	local/block file
not declared	in fun. outside fun.	any expression constant expr.	local/block program

Declaration of Pointers, Arrays, and Functions

Declaration	Meaning
long L;	L is a long variable
long *L;	L is a pointer to a long variable
long L[];	L is an array of longs
long L();	L is function returning a long value
long *L[];	L is an array of pointers to longs
long *L();	L is a function returning a pointer to a long value
long (*L)();	L is a pointer to a function returning a long value
long (*L)[];	L is a pointer to an array of longs

Structures

```
struct sexamp { int   ivar;
                long  lvar;
                int   bvar : 5; /* bit field */
                char  *msg;
              } instance1 = {2, 8L, 4, "Hi"};

struct sexamp   instance2, sarray[4], *sexamp_ptr[8];

   instance2.ivar = instance1.ivar;
   sarray[2].ivar = instance1.ivar;
  *sexamp_ptr[2] = &instance1;
 (*sexamp_ptr[2]).lvar = 5L;
   sexamp_ptr[2]->lvar = 5L;
```

Unions

```
union uexamp { int   ivar;
               long  lvar;
               float fvar;
             } uinstance1; /* cannot init. */

union uexamp   uinstance2, uarray[4], *uexamp_ptr[8];

   uinstance2.ivar = uinstance1.ivar;
   uarray[2].ivar = uinstance1.ivar;
  *uexamp_ptr[2] = &uinstance1;
 (*uexamp_ptr[2]).lvar = 5L;
   uexamp_ptr[2]->lvar = 5L;
```

Appendix G

Arrays and Pointers

```
int   i;
char a[20], *a_ptr;
char b[20][5];

  i = *(&i);


      a <--> &a[0]
   a[i] <--> (*(a+i))
 b[i][j] <--> (*(*(b+i)+j))

*a_ptr-- <--> *(a_ptr--)
```

Preprocessor Directives

#define - defines character substitution strings
           and macros

defined - used in the #if to test for definitions

#elif   - used as an else-if with the #if

#else   - used as an else with the #if

#endif - indicates end of a #if, #ifdef, #ifndef

#if   - tests constant values

#ifdef - tests for defined values

#ifndef - tests for undefined values

#include - includes source files

#line   - sets line numbers for symbolic debuggers

#undef - undefines a #define or command line
           definition

Statements

Statements	Comment/Format
;	(null statement)
break;	(ends do, for, switch, and while)
continue;	(used with do, for, and while)
do	do statement while (expression);
for	for(init,cont,bottom) statement
goto	goto label; label:

if	if (expression) if (expression)
	   statement statement
	                   else if
	                      statement
	                   else
	                      statement

return	return return expression;

switch	switch (integer-expression) {
	    case (integer1) : statement
	                   break;
	    case (integer2) : statement
	                   statement
	                   break;
	
	    default : statement
	}

while	while (expression) while () statement

Appendix G

comment	operator	direction	precedence	
Primary Expression	() [] -> . defined	→	1	HIGH
Unary	Post ++ --	→	2	
	Pre ++ -- ! ° - * + & (type) sizeof	←		
Multiplicative	* / %	→	3	
Additive	+ -	→	4	
Bit Shift	<< >>	→	5	
Relational	< <= > >=	→	6	
Equality	== !=	→	7	
AND	&	→	8	
exclusive OR	^	→	9	
inclusive OR	|	→	10	
logical AND	&&	→	11	
logical OR	||	→	12	
conditional	? :	←	13	
Assignment	= %= += -= *= /= >>= <<= &= ^= |=	←	14	
comma	,	→	15	LOW

SECTION
6

References and Resources

- **Books**
- **Periodicals**

Books

Digital Equipment Corporation. *Programming in VAX-11 C*. Maynard, MA: Digital, 1982.

> Digital Equipment Corporation's reference manual for programming in C on the VAX-11 C.

Feuer, Alan R. *The C Puzzle Book*. Englewood Cliffs, NJ: Prentice-Hall, 1982.

> In a niche by itself, this is a splendid book. Every C programmer should test his or her wits with this classic.

Harbison, Samuel P. and Guy L. Steele. *A C Reference Manual*. Englewood Cliffs, NJ: Prentice-Hall, 1984.

> The successor to *The C Programming Language*. This book is slightly flawed by blanket statements, but otherwise is an excellent reference.

Kelly, Al and Ira Pohl. *A Book On C*. Menlo Park, CA: Benjamin/Cummings, 1984.

> An excellent, introductory book that discusses a variety of application disciplines, from text processing to mathematics. This book contains dozens of valuable tables that reinforce the material and would make an excellent textbook.

Kernighan, Brian W. and Robert Pike. *The UNIX Programming Environment*. Englewood Cliffs, NJ: Prentice-Hall, 1984.

> Destined to be another classic for UNIX users. This book shows how to avoid any programming by using the UNIX utilities. If utilities cannot do the trick, then the book will show how to proceed.

Kernighan, Brian W. and Dennis M. Ritchie. *The C Programming Language*. Englewood Cliffs, NJ: Prentice-Hall, 1978.

> The seminal work on C by the creators of the language. This classic does not mention some of the subsequent extensions to the original language. While still useful, a beginner should consider combining an introductory book with Harbison and Steele's *A C Reference Manual*.

Kochan, Stephen G. *Programming in C*. Rochelle Park, NJ: Hayden, 1983.

> An excellent, introductory tutorial. Any language would be lucky to have such a book. Its treatment of structures is excellent.

Martin, Donald, Stephen Prata, *C Primer Plus*. Indianapolis, IN: Sams, 1984.

> A good, user-friendly, introductory book diminished by a few errors.

Plum, Thomas. *C Programming Guidelines*. Englewood Cliffs, NJ: Prentice-Hall, 1984.

> A treatise on good C-programming practices. Recommended reading for large C-programming projects.

Plum, Thomas. *Learning to Program In C*. Cardiff, NJ: Plum Hall, 1983.

> An introductory book now eclipsed by other introductory books in this bibliography.

Purdum, Jack. *C Programming Guide*. Indianapolis, IN: Que, 1983.

> A good, introductory book with routines coded in BASIC and in C for comparison.

MetaWare, *MetaWare C Language Reference Manual*. Santa Cruz: MetaWare, Inc.

> Tentatively titled, and still in production, this manual is a terse, formal and precise definition of the language and recommended for rigorous research. Check with MetaWare Inc. for availability.

Wortman, Leon A. and Thomas O. Sidebottom, *The C Programming Tutor*. New York: Brady, 1984.

> A solid, introductory book that makes a serious attempt to illustrate the use of C in real, intermediate-level applications. It has some splendid routines.

Periodicals

San Francisco, CA: *Computer Language*. Computer Language Publishing.

> An excellent monthly magazine on languages with regular columns discussing C.

Renton, WA: *UNIX Review*. Review Publications.

> An excellent monthly magazine on UNIX with a column discussing C.

Index